# COMP

## EXERCISES IN
## COMPREHENSION AND COMPOSITION

### L.G. ALEXANDER
AND
### EDWIN T. CORNELIUS, JR.

$ unit Church
190 Beverly Rd (Hyrith Burgen)
271 Ny Ave.         718) 287-4700
230 W 29 st              10-3

**LONGMAN INC.**
New York

COMP

**Library of Congress Cataloging in Publication Data**

Alexander, L.G.
    COMP, Exercises in Comprehension and Composition.

    Published (c1965) under title: A FIRST BOOK IN COM-
PREHENSION PRECIS AND COMPOSITION.
      1.  English language—Textbooks for foreigners.
2.  English language—Composition and exercises.
I.  Cornelius, Edwin T., joint author.  II.  Title.
PE1128.A456      1978      428'.4'3      78-16637
**ISBN** 0 582 79703 9

First printing 1978

5   4

*Illustrations:* Mike Quon
*Cover design:* Suzanne M. D'Alleinne

 Longman Inc.
19 West 44th Street
New York, New York 10036

Distributed in the United Kingdom by Longman Group Ltd.,
Longman House, Burnt Mill, Harlow, Essex CM20 2JE, England,
and by associated companies, branches and representatives
throughout the world.

Printed in the U.S.A.

# Contents

# Introduction

The purpose of this book is to provide guidance and training to students in the development of writing skills in English. The material contained here may be used as an adjunct to a basic course series, or it may be used as the principal textbook for special remedial and refresher courses. Since the four sections of the book deliberately parallel different stages of learning from beginning to low advanced levels, the book may be used over a two- to three-year period as the writing syllabus for any basic course in ongoing programs. When used as the main textbook for special remedial or refresher courses, the four sections provide sufficient material for approximately six months of intensive study.

## General Aims

The development of writing skills is often neglected at beginning levels of instruction. Although grammar texts and drill books used in general language work include writing exercises, students usually find it difficult to transfer what they have learned through these exercises to later assignments for writing continuous prose in English. The basic problem, of course, is that students need a great deal of guided practice in writing sentences and in joining them together to form continuous prose.

This book is based on the idea that at early stages of learning, the development of *reading comprehension skills* and *elementary writing skills* are complementary activities. The aim, then, should be to teach paragraph writing and composition through the use of reading comprehension exercises. That is, students should be required to derive specific information from a given reading selection and then to put this information together in an orderly way to form a paragraph of their own.

In the first three sections of this book, students will learn the essentials of writing simple, compound and complex sentences. At the same time, students will be trained to join sentences together to form paragraph summaries of assigned reading passages. The amount of help the students are given to carry out assignments is gradually diminished from section to section. In the final section of the book—representing more advanced stages—reading comprehension exercises and writing assignments are treated as separate activities and students are asked to carry out independent writing assignments. At this stage, students should be able to write simple forms of summaries and essays without assistance from the teacher.

### Grading

The material has been carefully graded, from the point of view of both structure and vocabulary.

*Structure* A full listing of the structures which the student will be expected to use is given in the introductory notes to the teacher which precede Section 1. These notes will enable teachers to tell at a glance whether or not their students are ready for this book.

*Vocabulary* The approximate vocabulary range in each section is as follows:

| | |
|---|---|
| Section 1 | 600 words |
| Section 2 | 1,000 words |
| Section 3 | 1,400 words |
| Section 4 | 1,800 words |

The reading passages presented in the book increase in length and complexity as students progress from section to section.

## Introductions to the Sections

Each section is preceded by separate introductory notes to teachers and to students. In early sections, the instructions intended for students have been simplified somewhat to enable students to work through the materials on their own. Satisfactory results with these materials will be obtained only if the instructions are carefully followed.

# Section 1

## THE SIMPLE SENTENCE

### To the teacher

#### 1. Aims

(a) To enable the student to write simple sentences.

(b) To enable the student to put these sentences together to form a continuous paragraph.

(c) To help the student grasp basic word order in English sentences: Subject/Verb/Complement and/or Verb modifiers.

#### 2. How the student should work

The questions on the passages have been designed to elicit *simple* sentences from the student. These sentences should be written in a logical sequence as *continuous prose* so that the student's answers to the questions will form a single paragraph which, at the same time, will be a summary of the passage. Each writing assignment, therefore, will provide the student with simultaneous practice in comprehension, summarizing and composition.

(a) **Question and Answer** Students will be expected to derive all their information from the reading passages. The questions given in the book do not always follow each passage closely. The reason for this is that the aim of these exercises is to encourage students to use their own words.

Teachers should insist on a full answer to each question. Short answers, such as "Yes, he did," "No, he did not," etc., should not be given. To discourage students from writing short answers, most questions beginning with "Did" (or any other auxiliary) have been phrased as follows:

Did the man go into the house or not?
Or: Did the man go into the house, or did he stay out in the front yard?

(b) **Word Order**  In order to help students grasp the basic Subject/Verb/Complement and/or Verb modifiers pattern of an English sentence, the teacher should make every effort at this stage to discourage students from separating a subject from its verb, or a verb from its complement and modifiers. (The only exception to this rule will be in the case of adverbs of frequency, *always, ever, never, often,* etc.) The teacher should point out that time expressions (*in the morning, last week, yesterday,* etc.) may be placed *before* the subject or *after* the complement.

For example, the answer to a question might be:

| Subject | Verb | Complement | Verb Modifier |
|---------|------|------------|---------------|
| I | met | George | last week. |

Or:

| Verb modifier | Subject | Verb | Complement |
|---------------|---------|------|------------|
| Last week | I | met | George. |

The only exception to this rule will be where an adverb of frequency must be included in the answer in connection with the simple present tense:

| Subject | | Verb | Complement |
|---------|---|------|------------|
| I | *often* | meet | George. |

At the outset, however, changing the position of a time expression should be the only experimenting with word order that students should allow themselves. They should be told that the position of modifiers in their responses to questions will normally depend on the word order of the question.

### 3. Vocabulary range

At this stage, students should have a passive vocabulary of about 800 words. The actual range is 600 words. The passages are based on the most commonly used 600 words in the English language (with only a small number of exceptions). The reading passages have been graded in order of increasing difficulty.

### 4. Length of each passage

Approximately 80 words. Each passage consists of one paragraph.

### 5. Length of summaries

Approximately 50 words. The number of words for each summary will vary. The word limit for each summary has been precalculated and is given with each assignment.

### 6. Structures

The reading passages contain simple and compound sentences, but very few complex sentences. The word order follows a simple pattern and the sentences are short and easy to understand. Active verb constructions have been used throughout Section 1.

The following is a brief summary of the main structures students will be expected to use (as distinct from those the students will be required to recognize):

(a) **Articles** Elementary uses of *a* and *the*.

(b) **Nouns** Forming the plural with "s" or "es" (exceptions: money, advice).

(c) **Pronouns** Personal and possessive. The use of possessive *'s*. The use of *one* in place of a noun (e.g., "the new one").

(d) **Adjectives** Cardinal and ordinal numbers. Position before a noun. Regular comparison: *-er than, -est.* Irregular comparison: *more . . . than.*

(e) **Verbs**

Tenses: Simple present, Simple past (regular and irregular), Present continuous (also, to indicate future time), Past continuous, Present perfect, Future with *will, be going to.*

Auxiliary verbs, Modals, and Verb expressions: *will/ would, can/could, have to/must.* Verb + *begin to, decide to, learn how to, like to, start to, try to, want to.* (Exception: *let* + verb.) Expressions: *be afraid of, be in charge of, call a number, charge to an account, feel angry, go on a trip, go places, tell a lie, tell the truth.*

Irregular verbs: *be, become, begin, break, bring, build, buy, catch, come, cost, drive, eat, feel, find, fly, forget, get, give, go, have, hear, hold, keep, know, lead, leave, let, lie, lose, make, meet, ring, run, say, see, sing, sit, speak, spend, take, tell, think, throw, wake, wear,* and *write.*

(f) **Adverbs** Formation with "-ly" (*carefully, slowly,* etc.). Formation with "-ily" (*heavily*). (Exception: late.)

(g) **Prepositions** *about, across, after, along, around, for, from, in, into, of, on, out, to, towards, through, up.*

(h) **Miscellaneous Grammatical Points**
The use of *ago*
*Anything/nothing, something/nothing, anyone/no one*
*Old* (seventeen years old)
Days of the week, months, seasons
The date
Verbs with 2 objects: to give someone something
to give something to someone
*Ever/never* (question and answer)
Impersonal subject: *It is/was . . .*
*There is/was . . .*

*Kind of/kinds of* (+ agreement of noun)
*Much/many/a lot of/few*
Negatives with *do* and *did*
*Say/tell*
Telling time
*Too/very*

(i) **Expressions** *this morning, in the evening, last Saturday, the other day, the next day, one night, in the winter, next year, at first, at last, finally, in the end, just then, a long time, a short time, each other, for lunch, for tea, a lot of trouble, by air, next door, in a row.*

## To the student

There are twenty reading passages in this section. You will answer questions on each passage. At the same time, you will learn how to write short, simple sentences. In each exercise you will put these sentences together to form a short paragraph.

Before you begin Section 1, read these instructions:

### How to Work

1. Read the passage carefully two or three times.
2. Write an answer to each question. Each answer must be a complete sentence.
3. Your answers must follow each other. All the sentences together will then make *a complete paragraph.*
4. Read through your work and correct your mistakes.
5. Count the number of words in your paragraph. Put this number in parentheses ( ) at the end of your paragraph.
6. Give your paragraph a title (make one up).

Now study this example carefully, and then try to do the exercises in the same way by yourself.

### Example

Mr. Johnson looked at his watch. It was seven-thirty. He got out of bed quickly. Then he washed and

dressed. He was late as usual, so he did not have time for breakfast. He ran all the way to the bus stop and
5 arrived there just in time to catch his bus. Mr. Johnson never eats anything in the morning. He always says to his friends at the office: "It's nice to have breakfast in the morning, but it's nicer to lie in bed!"

## Summary

Your answer must not be more than 46 words.

1. What time did Mr. Johnson get up?
2. Was he early, or was he late?
3. Did he have time for breakfast or not?
4. Did he run all the way to the bus stop, or did he walk part of the way?
5. Did he just catch the bus, or did he miss the bus?
6. Does Mr. Johnson ever eat anything in the morning?
7. Does he prefer to have breakfast or to lie in bed?

## Answer

(Title:) *No Breakfast*

Mr. Johnson got up at seven-thirty. He was late. He did not have time for breakfast. He ran all the way to the bus stop. He just caught the bus. Mr. Johnson never eats anything in the morning. He prefers to lie in
5 bed.

(44 Words)

I have a friend in the U.S. His name is Don Adams. I know him very well, but I have never met him. We write to each other all the time. My letters are very short. It is still hard for me to write in English. I
5 received a letter from Don yesterday. It made me very happy. He is coming to my country for a visit next summer. We are going to see each other for the first time.

**Summary**

Your answer must not be more than 51 words.

1. Where does your friend Don Adams live?
2. Have you ever met him?
3. What do you both do?
4. Are your letters short or long?
5. Is it hard for you to write in English, or is it easy?
6. What will Don do next summer?
7. Will you see each other for the first time or not?

2  I am learning how to drive a car. A week ago I had my first lesson. Yesterday my instructor took me out on some busy streets. They were full of cars and people. I drove very slowly and carefully, but I was
5 afraid the whole time. Finally the lesson was over and I went home. I felt very tired. I have learned quite a bit, but I still have a lot to learn.

**Summary**

Your answer must not be more than 44 words.

1. What are you learning to do?
2. When did you have your first lesson?
3. Where did your instructor take you yesterday?
4. Did you drive fast and carelessly, or did you drive slowly and carefully?
5. How did you feel after the lesson?
6. Do you still have a lot to learn or not?

**3** Our summer vacation lasts three months. During the last week of vacation, we get ready for school. We buy pencils, pens, book covers, notebooks and notebook paper. On the first day of school, we see all
5 our old friends again and we talk about our summer experiences. After that we go to class. It is so hard to keep quiet and pay attention. Our teacher always says with a laugh, "You forget more in three months than you learn in a year!"

**Summary**

Your answer must not be more than 56 words.

1. How long does your summer vacation last?
2. When do you prepare for school?
3. When do you see all your old friends again?
4. What do you talk about?
5. Where do you go then?
6. What does your teacher always say?

**4** On holidays nobody likes staying at home. People go on picnics, take trips or visit friends and relatives. We have quite a few parks with good campgrounds in this part of the country and my friends and I often go
5 camping. Sometimes the parks are crowded, but we do not mind. We go on hikes and explore the country around us. After dark, we sit around an open fire and talk for hours. We can forget all our problems and enjoy the outdoors.

**Summary**

Your answer must not be more than 53 words.

1. Do people like to go places on holidays, or do they like to stay at home?
2. What do they do?
3. Where do you and your friends often go?
4. Do you always stay close to your campsite, or do you go on hikes and explore the countryside?
5. What do you do after dark?
6. Do you think about all your problems, or can you forget everything and enjoy the outdoors?

It is January 10. Jane is eleven years old today. She is wearing a pretty new dress. It is blue and white. Jane is having a party today and she is expecting all her friends to come. They are going to be here in just
5 a little while. They are going to bring a lot of presents with them. Jane's mother has made a lot of good things to eat and drink. Jane and her friends are going to play games, sing, dance and listen to music. They will have a good time together.

**Summary**

Your answer must not be more than 48 words.

1. What is the date today?
2. Whose birthday is it?
3. How old is she?
4. Is Jane wearing a new dress, or is she wearing an old one?
5. Is she having a party or not?
6. When will her friends arrive?
7. What are Jane and her friends going to do at the party?

It is still winter, but on Sunday the weather was beautiful. We decided to go on a trip to the coast. The

sun was bright and warm, but we did not go into the
water. It was too cold. Instead, we walked along the
5 beach and looked at the ocean and the rocks. In the
evening we returned home. Then the temperature
dropped and it began to snow. So we sat around the
fireplace. We did not mind the weather at all.

**Summary**

Your answer must not be more than 45 words.

1. Is it still winter or is it summer?
2. Did you go to the coast on Sunday or not?
3. Where did you walk?
4. What did you look at?
5. When did you go back home?
6. What happened then?
7. What did you do?

**7**

The young man heard a cry and turned around, but
he could not see anybody. At the same moment, a boy
ran up to him and pointed towards the river. They
both ran along the river bank and after a short time,
5 they saw a girl in the water. The girl was holding on to
a log, but the current was fast and it was carrying her
away. The man acted quickly. He pulled off his shoes
and his coat, jumped into the water and saved the
girl's life.

**Summary**

Your answer must not be more than 43 words.

1. What did the young man hear?
2. Who ran up to him just then?
3. Where did the boy point?
4. What did they both do?
5. What did they both see?
6. Did the man act quickly or not?
7. Did he rescue the girl, or did the girl drown?

 Last weekend I flew for the first time in my life. I generally travel by bus or by car. It seems safer to me. But this was an unexpected business trip. At the beginning, I did not feel very happy about flying. This
5 feeling did not last long. The trip was very exciting. We were soon flying high in the sky. It was a clear day and the view of mountains, fields and rivers was beautiful. I enjoyed my short and comfortable flight very much.

**Summary**

Your answer must not be more than 43 words.

1. When did you first travel by air?
2. Was it an unexpected business trip or not?
3. How did you feel at first?
4. Did this feeling soon pass or not?
5. What was the trip like?
6. Was the view of mountains, fields and rivers beautiful or not?
7. Was the short flight comfortable, or was it uncomfortable?

 Mr. and Mrs. Allen go grocery shopping on Saturday mornings. Mr. Allen never enjoys these trips. Mrs.

Allen does the shopping and he sits in the car and waits for her. This morning there were a lot of people 5 and it took Mrs. Allen longer than usual. An hour went by and finally a man came up to Mr. Allen. "Excuse me," he said, "is your name Allen? Your wife is waiting for you at the check-out counter. She doesn't have enough money for the groceries!"

### Summary

Your answer must not be more than 47 words.

1. What do Mr. and Mrs. Allen do every Saturday morning?
2. Does Mr. Allen enjoy it or not?
3. Does he do the shopping, or does he sit in the car and wait for his wife?
4. Did Mrs. Allen have enough money to pay for the groceries this morning or not?
5. What did Mrs. Allen want her husband to do?

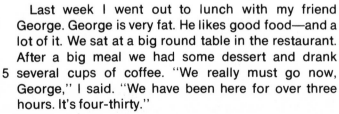

Last week I went out to lunch with my friend George. George is very fat. He likes good food—and a lot of it. We sat at a big round table in the restaurant. After a big meal we had some dessert and drank 5 several cups of coffee. "We really must go now, George," I said. "We have been here for over three hours. It's four-thirty."

"What do you mean?" asked George in surprise. "We can't leave now. It's nearly time for dinner!"

## Summary

Your answer must not be more than 49 words.

1. Did you and George go to a restaurant for lunch or for dinner?
2. Is George fat, or is he thin?
3. Does he like a lot of good food or not?
4. Did you eat a big meal, or did you eat a light one?
5. How long did you stay at the restaurant?
6. What time was it?
7. Did George want to leave, or did he want to stay?
8. Was it nearly time for breakfast, or was it time for dinner?

 I worked as a mailman for a short time. However, I am afraid of dogs and I had a lot of trouble. One day I tried to deliver some letters to a big house. I started to open the gate and all of a sudden a huge dog ran
5 toward me. It growled and barked at me, so I threw the letters over the fence. The dog picked them up and carried them into the house. The dog was a better mailman than I was!

## Summary

Your answer must not be more than 58 words.

1. Did you work as a mailman for a long time or for a short time?
2. Did you find the work easy, or did you find it difficult?
3. Do you like dogs, or are you afraid of them?
4. Where did you have to deliver some letters one day?
5. Would the dog at the house let you go through the gate or not?
6. Where did you throw the letters?
7. Where did the dog take them?

## 12

It rained a lot last winter and the little stream near our house turned into a big river. It overflowed and flooded all the fields around our house. Luckily, the water did not reach any of the houses in our area, but
5 the flood washed away our beautiful wooden bridge. The bridge was more than forty years old and we were sorry to lose it. We are building a new one now, but it will never be the same.

### Summary

Your answer must not be more than 47 words.

1. When did the little stream near your house become a big river?
2. What did it do to the fields all around your house?
3. Did the water reach any of the houses in your area or not?
4. What happened to your old wooden bridge?
5. What are you doing now?

## 13

"Did you buy anything overseas?" asked the Customs officer.

"Just a few small souvenirs," answered the lady. "I didn't buy anything of value."

5 "Would you open this suitcase, please?" asked the officer.

"Of course," said the lady, "but it's only full of dirty clothes."

"That doesn't matter," replied the officer. "I'm used
10 to that."

At that moment, the lady's daughter, a little girl of five, said, "Oh, be careful! Don't touch my mommy's old blue coat! Her new gold watch is in the pocket. You might break it!"

### Summary

Your answer must not be more than 49 words.

1. Did the lady tell the Customs officer a lie, or did she tell him the truth?

2. Did she say, "I didn't buy anything of value," or did she say "I bought something valuable"?
3. Did the officer want her to open a suitcase or not?
4. What did the lady's daughter say just then?
5. Did the child tell the officer the truth or not?
6. What was there in the coat pocket?

The children next door often play baseball in the yard and sometimes break my bedroom window. Last Saturday afternoon I stayed at home and watched TV. After a while, I closed my eyes and went to sleep. A
5 sound at the door made me wake up suddenly. A little boy appeared at the door.

"Not one of my windows again!" I said.

"Oh, no!" answered the boy. "Your window was open this time and our ball is in your bedroom. Can
10 we get it, please?"

**Summary**

Your answer must not be more than 52 words.

1. Where do the children next door often play baseball?
2. What do they sometimes break?
3. Where did you spend the afternoon last Saturday?
4. Who came to the door?
5. What did he want to do?
6. Where was it?
7. Did they break your window this time or not?
8. Was the window open, or was it closed?

Mrs. Mills often spends too much money on clothes. She does not need new clothes, but she loves buying them. Yesterday she saw a beautiful coat in a store window. She went in and tried it on. It was just
5 the right size, but it was very expensive. Mrs. Mills did not have enough money with her, so she charged it to

her account. Then she took the coat home and showed it to her husband. After that, she showed him the sales slip for $200. He liked the coat very much,
10 but he didn't like the price!

## Summary

Your answer must not be more than 50 words.

1. Does Mrs. Mills often waste money on clothes or not?
2. What did she see in a store window yesterday?
3. Was it too small, too large or just the right size?
4. Did Mrs. Mills charge the coat to her account, or did she pay cash for it?
5. Did she leave the coat in the store, or did she take it home and show it to her husband?
6. Did he like the price or not?
7. How much did the coat cost?

There was a great deal of excitement in town the other day. A horse got out of a field and came into town on its own. It walked across the school grounds and through several busy streets. Then it lay down in
5 the middle of Main Street opposite the post office. All traffic stopped. Quite a few people tried to lead it away, but no one could move it. Finally, a farmer appeared. He called to it. It got up and he led it away.

**Summary**

Your answer must not be more than 45 words.

1. What caused a lot of excitement in town the other day?
2. Where did it go?
3. Where did it lie down?
4. Could anyone move it or not?
5. Who led it away finally?

## 17

The telephone rang and I picked up the receiver.

"Hello," I said.

"Hello," said a voice. "This is Bill. Is Betty there?"

"I'm sorry," I said, "you have the wrong number."

5   A few seconds later the telephone rang again. Just as I suspected, it was Bill. "You've dialed the wrong number two times in a row," I explained.

Then the phone rang a third time. This made me angry. I spoke in a loud voice, "Hello, Bill. This is
10 Betty."

For a moment there was complete silence. Then someone said, "What's the *matter* with you, Tom?"

It was my mother!

**Summary**

Your answer must not be more than 50 words.

1. How many times did a strange man call?
2. What was his name?
3. Did he want to talk to you or to Betty?
4. Did he dial the wrong number once, or did he dial the wrong number two times in a row?
5. Did the phone ring a third time or not?
6. Did you feel angry, or did you feel pleased?
7. What did you say?
8. Was it Bill or not?
9. Who was it?

**18** Mr. Dawson is the head of a large company. The other day, he was talking to his son.

"Well, Peter," he said, "you finished college five months ago. You really should start thinking about the future. There are fine opportunities in the business for a bright young man like you. You will gradually gain experience. Who knows . . . in twenty years you may even have a position like mine. Of course, a little hard work will be necessary."

10 "Yes, I know," replied Peter, "but I don't want to go into business. I want to be an actor!"

**Summary**

Your answer must not be more than 52 words.

1. What is Mr. Dawson in charge of?
2. The other day, was he giving his son some advice or not?
3. When did Peter graduate from college?
4. Did his father want him to come into the business or not?
5. What would Peter have to do?
6. Does he like the idea or not?
7. What does he want to become?

**19** It was very dark. Two men were making their way slowly through the woods. Snow was lying on the ground and a cold wind was blowing. They noticed a light through the trees and soon came to a cabin. An old man immediately invited them to come in. He seemed to be a strange fellow, but he spoke kindly and offered them hot soup and bread. The men remained there until morning. Then the old man led them to the nearest town, but he would not accept any money for his help.

**Summary**

Your answer must not be more than 50 words.

1. Where were two men walking one cold, dark night?
2. What did they find?
3. Who lived there?
4. Did he ask them in, or did he tell them to go away?
5. Did he give them a simple meal, or did he give them nothing at all?
6. Did the men stay there all night, or did they leave immediately?
7. Where did the old man take them the next day?

Our old church building was in very bad condition. So last March we decided to build a new one at the top of a hill just south of town. We used many different kinds of materials. We built the walls of stone and
5 glass, and the heavy doors of wood and metal. From the front steps of the church, there is a wonderful view. You can see the town and the entire countryside for miles around. People from all parts of the state visit the church. It is such an interesting structure.

**Summary**

Your answer must not be more than 41 words.

1. When did you decide to build a new church?
2. Did you build it at the top of a hill, or did you build it at the foot of a hill?
3. Did you use only stone or many different materials?
4. Is there a good view or a poor view of the town and countryside from the top?
5. Do a lot of people visit the church, or do very few people visit it?

## THE COMPOUND SENTENCE

### To the teacher

#### 1. Aims

  (a)  To enable the student to write compound sentences.

  (b)  To enable the student to put these sentences together to form a continuous paragraph.

  (c)  To help the student gain experience in handling conjunctions and connecting phrases.

  (d)  To provide additional exercises in writing simple sentences (practiced in Section 1).

#### 2. How the student should work

The questions on the reading passages have been designed to elicit compound sentences from the student. As in the previous section, these sentences should be written in a logical sequence as continuous prose. The student's answers to the questions should form a single paragraph.

  (a)  **Question and Answer**  The questions in this section differ in one important respect from those given in Section 1. In order to be able to write a compound sentence of their own, students will have to answer two or sometimes three questions in a single sentence. The conjunctions the students should use are given in parentheses at the end of each series of questions.

The following is an example of a series of questions of this sort:

> Who did you call after breakfast? Did anyone answer? When did you call again? *(but) (so)*

The answer to these questions should be written in one sentence, using the conjunctions given in parentheses:

> After breakfast I called my friend Tim, *but* no one answered, *so* I called again at noon.

(b) **Word Order** The basic Subject/Verb/Complement and/or Verb modifier pattern should again be closely followed. In this section, however, the Subject will not always be a single word, but will frequently take the form of a phrase; for example:

| Subject | Verb | Complement | Verb modifier |
|---|---|---|---|
| **A man in a black coat** | **bought** | **a ticket** | **at the station.** |

### 3. Vocabulary range

The student's passive vocabulary should be about 1,200 words. The actual range (taking into account the words used in the previous section) is about 1,000 words. The reading passages have been graded in order of increasing difficulty.

### 4. Length of each passage

150 to 160 words (single paragraphs).

### 5. Length of summaries

70 to 85 words. The word limit given with each assignment should be strictly observed.

### 6. Structures

Though the active voice has again been employed throughout this section, the reading passages now contain complex sentences, in addition to simple and compound. Students will also be expected to use Past Perfect constructions. They should, furthermore, be completely familiar with usage rules governing the sequence of tenses.

The conjunctions the students will be expected to use are as follows: *after, and, and now, and so, and then, both . . . and, but, however, neither . . . nor, not only . . . but also, not only . . . but . . . as well, now, so, so that, then.*

Connecting words and phrases the students will be expected to use are the following: *the next day, just then, suddenly, all of a sudden, at that moment, at this point, from there, last week, meanwhile, one night, one day, finally, there, this, some days later, immediately, soon, for an instant, beyond, after, this time, in this way.*

## To the student

There are twenty reading passages in this section, and you will again answer questions on each passage. You will learn how to join simple sentences together with words like *and, but, so, then,* etc. We call "joining words" of this sort *conjunctions.* Conjunctions help us join different ideas together to make *compound* sentences.

Before you begin the readings in this section, read these instructions:

### How to Work

1.  Read each passage carefully two or three times.
2.  Write a full answer to each question. When you find two or three questions together, join your answers with the conjunctions given in parentheses. Each answer you write must be a complete sentence.
3.  Your answers to the questions must follow each other. All the sentences together will then make a complete paragraph.

4. Read through your work and correct your mistakes.
5. Count the number of words in your paragraph. Do not go over the word limit given in the book. At the end of your paragraph, give the number of words you have used.
6. Give your paragraph a title.

Now study this example carefully, and then try to do the exercises in the same way by yourself.

### Example

Nobody likes staying at home on a holiday weekend —especially if the weather is good. Last Fourth of July we decided to spend the day in the country. The only difficulty was that thousands of other people had ex-
5 actly the same idea. We moved out of town slowly in bumper-to-bumper traffic, but at last we were able to turn off on a quiet side road and, after some time, stopped near an old farmhouse. We had brought plenty of food with us in a big picnic basket and we
10 got the basket out of the car. We spread things out on the ground near a path at the foot of a hill. Everything was ready now, so we sat down. It was very peaceful in the cool grass—until we heard bells ringing at the top of the hill. What we saw made us pick up our
15 things and run back to the car as quickly as possible. There was a flock of a hundred or more sheep coming down the trail directly towards us!

### Summary

Your answer must not be more than 80 words.

1. Where did we decide to drive last Fourth of July?
2. Were there a lot of cars on the highway, or were there only a few? Did it take us a long time to get out of town or not? *(so)*
3. What did we get out of the car? Where did we sit down? *(and)*

4.	What did we hear soon afterwards? Where did we have to run back to? *(and)*
5.	What was coming down the path?

**Answer**

*A Day in the Country*

Last Fourth of July we decided to drive into the country. There were a lot of cars on the highway, *so* it took us a long time to get out of town. We got the picnic basket out of the car *and* sat down on the ground near a path at the foot of a hill. Soon afterwards, we heard bells ringing *and* we had to run back to the car. A flock of sheep was coming down the path!

(80 Words)

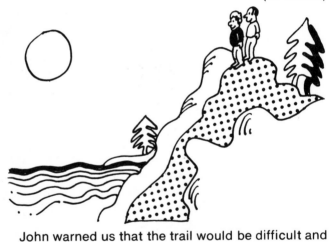

John warned us that the trail would be difficult and that we would have to cross several dangerous spots to reach the top of Neahkanie Mountain. At first we made our way up the trail easily and felt that John had
5	been exaggerating, but later we changed our minds. The trail ended abruptly, and there was only a ledge four or five inches wide that circled on around the mountain. We moved to the edge cautiously and looked over. There was a drop straight down of a
10	thousand feet or more. As we inched along the narrow ledge, we felt as if the ledge was going to crumble at

any minute. It was quite a relief to reach the other side and find a wide trail again. From the top there was a beautiful view of the coastline, and for a few minutes
15  we put out of our minds the thought of having to face the ledge again.

## Summary

Your answer must not be more than 85 words.

1. Did you think the trail up the mountain was easy or difficult? Did you change your minds later on or not? *(but)*
2. Did the trail go on for several miles, or did it end abruptly? Was there just a ten-foot drop over the edge, or was there a thousand-foot drop? *(and)*
3. Did you walk on a wide trail, or did you have to walk along a narrow ledge? Did you feel that the ledge was solid, or did you feel as if the ledge was going to crumble at any minute? *(and)*
4. Was it a relief to reach the other side or not?
5. How was the view from the top? Did you know you had to walk along the ledge again on the way down or not? *(but)*

22    After returning to the surface, the diver told the captain that he had found a metal safe in the sunken ship, but he said that it would be impossible to cut it open underwater. The captain decided that the best
5  thing to do would be to blow the door off the safe. The diver went down again with a number of explosives which he fastened to the door of the safe, and then he came up immediately. After a few minutes, the explosives were set off electrically, sending up a
10  shower of water. When the surface of the water settled again, the diver descended for a third time to examine the contents of the safe. The explosion had torn away the door. In the lamplight, he caught sight of shining metal. Closer examination showed that
15  there were neat piles of gold bars inside the safe. Very

excited now, the diver took one of the bars and returned once more to the waiting ship above.

## Summary

Your answer must not be more than 69 words.

1. What did the diver find in the wreck? Could he open it or not? *(but)*
2. Did he go down again or not? What did he take with him? *(and)*
3. Did he return to the ship above once more, or did he stay underwater? Where did he go after the underwater explosion? *(and then)*
4. What did he see inside the safe this time?
5. What did he take? Did he return to the surface at once, or did he stay near the sunken ship? *(and)*

The train I was traveling on was already half an hour late. I had planned to arrive in Chicago at 7:10 in time to catch the 7:50 train to St. Louis—but there was no hope of that now. I explained the situation to the
5 conductor who advised me to get off at the stop before Union Station and take a taxi. When the time came, he even helped me with my luggage. He wished me good luck as I jumped off, and a few minutes later I was racing towards Union Station in a taxi. It was
10 almost 7:50 when we stopped outside the station. I paid the driver quickly, grabbed my bags and hurried inside.

"The St. Louis train . . .?" was all I had time to say to the first porter I saw. You can imagine my disappoint-
15 ment when he pointed to a train that was just moving out of the station!

## Summary

Your answer must not be more than 73 words.

1. Was your train to Chicago going to arrive on time or not? What had you planned to do there? *(and)*

2. Were you worried or not? Who did you turn to for help? *(so)*
3. What did he tell you to do?
4. Did you take his advice or not? Were you half an hour late, or did you manage to get to the station by 7:50? *(and)*
5. Did you rush into the station, or did you wait outside for a few minutes? Was the train standing in the station, or was it just leaving? Did you catch it, or did you miss it? *(but) (and)*

**24** My friend Steve is not very mechanically inclined. Driving along a highway one dark night, he suddenly had a flat tire. Even worse, he discovered that he did not have a spare in the trunk! Steve waved to passing
5  cars and trucks, but not one of them stopped. Half an hour passed and he was almost desperate. Finally somebody stopped. It was a car just like his, and to his surprise, a well-dressed young lady got out. Steve was terribly disappointed. How could someone like this
10  possibly help him? The lady offered him her own spare tire, but Steve had to explain that he had never changed a tire in his life! She went to work at once and changed the tire in just a few minutes while Steve looked on in admiration.

## Summary

Your answer must not be more than 80 words.

1. What sort of person is Steve?
2. Did he have a flat tire one night or not? Did he have a spare tire or not? *(and)*
3. Did he wave to passing cars for ten minutes or for half an hour? Did somebody finally stop or not? Was he pleased or disappointed to find that it was a young lady? *(and) (but)*
4. What did she offer him? Did he know how to change the tire or not? What did she have to do? *(but) (so)*
5. What did Steve do while she was changing it?

Last year we visited a large modern factory where they make glass. We first saw workmen mixing sand and other materials together in certain proportions. Then they added some broken glass to the mixture,
5 since apparently this helps to melt the mixture. They then fed the mixture into an extremely hot oven. At the far end of the oven, a stream of liquid glass poured out. At that point, some men lowered a metal frame into the liquid. As the frame came back up, it pulled
10 away a hot sheet of glass. Special rollers then took hold of the frame at either side and raised it upwards. Our guide told us that at this stage it was necessary for the glass to cool down slowly to give it strength. After the sheet of glass cooled down, another
15 machine cut it into big pieces which the workmen stored away. The glass was now ready for use.

## Summary

Your answer must not be more than 75 words.

1. What kind of factory did we visit last year?
2. What did workmen do with a mixture of sand and other materials?

3. What came out at one end of the oven? What did a metal frame pull up? *(and)*
4. Did the glass cool down, or did it stay hot? Did workmen cut it into small pieces, or did a machine cut it into big pieces? *(after)*
5. Was the glass now ready for use or not? What did the workmen do with it? *(and)*

It was the ambition of an eleven-year-old boy in Kansas City, Kansas, to be a railroad engineer. Born without arms, he had been to special schools where he learned to use his feet as "hands." He spent all his
5 spare time watching trains and one day his dreams came true. Seeing a deserted engine in the railroad yards, the boy climbed in. He had no difficulty in starting it up with his feet. Soon he was traveling along at thirty miles an hour. Brakemen in the yards
10 could not see anybody in the cab, so they reported the runaway engine to the trainmaster. Meanwhile the boy reached the Missouri border, stopped the engine himself and then started backing it up. When he was near his starting point, the trainmaster caught up with
15 the engine and jumped aboard. At first he was very angry, but he smiled when the boy said simply, "I like trains."

"Well, I'm glad you don't like planes!" answered the trainmaster.

**Summary**

Your answer must not be more than 83 words.

1. What had an eleven-year-old boy without arms learned to do?
2. What was his ambition?
3. What did he see one day? Did he start it up or not? Did he run it as far as the Missouri border or not? *(and not only . . . but)*

4. Did he get out then, or did he start backing it up? Who jumped aboard the engine soon afterwards? *(but)*
5. What did the boy say?
6. Did the trainmaster smile or not? What did he say? *(and)*

**27**      I always have a difficult time choosing presents. My imagination never seems to get beyond ties, handkerchiefs or perfume, but strangely enough, it did not take me long to decide on my wife's birthday
5 present. For the first time in my life I had a good idea —I would buy her a stereo record player. At the party, she suggested that I unpack it and put on some records. I set it up but it refused to work, so I decided I would try to fix it. Soon a crowd gathered to watch
10 me, and I could hear all sorts of "helpful" suggestions like "Try winding it up!" "The speakers are upside down!", etc. All of a sudden I realized the problem and I felt rather stupid—I had not plugged it in, but now I had to wait until nobody was looking. When the music
15 started, I heard somebody say to my wife, "Your husband's a genius! He fixed it!"

**Summary**

Your answer must not be more than 80 words.

1. Is it always easy for you to choose presents, or do you find it difficult? Did it take you very long to decide on your wife's birthday present or not? *(but)*
2. What did you buy her?
3. What did she ask you to do during the party?
4. Did the guests watch or not? Did they make "helpful" suggestions or not? Did it start playing, or did it refuse to work? *(and) (but)*
5. What did you realize all of a sudden?

6.  Did it still refuse to work, or did the music start a few minutes later? Did anybody find out what had really happened or not? *(and)*

When the woman opened the door, she guessed at once that the man was an escaped convict. There was mud on his face and on his torn clothes. He wanted to know if he could use the telephone. He told her that a
5   "friend" had asked him to make a call. She immediately asked what the friend's name was, but he replied that he had forgotten. This made the woman even more suspicious. She knew that there had been a prison break at Huntsville the night before. Deciding
10  not to take the risk, she closed the door in the man's face. For days she wondered whether she had done the right thing—until she related the incident to a neighbor. Her neighbor exclaimed, "Oh, that explains what happened the other night! Henry's car broke
15  down not far from your place. The driver of another car offered to help, so Henry sent him to your house to call me in Huntsville."

**Summary**

Your answer must not be more than 84 words.

1.  What did the man at the door appear to be?
2.  Who did he say had told him to come there? Could he remember the friend's name or not? *(but)*
3.  Did this make the woman suspicious or not? Did she let the man in, or did she refuse to let him in? *(so)*
4.  Did she relate the incident to a neighbor several days later or not? Was she surprised at her neighbor's response or not? *(and)*
5.  Did the neighbor explain that her car or her husband's car had broken down that night? Had he sent the man to the woman's house to use the phone or not? *(and that)*

 I always settle down comfortably in a barber chair and listen patiently to the barber. He explains the present political situation, women's fashions, or tells jokes which I have heard at least a dozen times
5 already. In twenty minutes I get a haircut and an amazing amount of information as well. But last week our conversation was cut short. We heard loud cries of "Fire!" coming from upstairs. Customers and barbers rushed out of the shop immediately. We were
10 certainly a funny sight to people on the street! I had a white sheet around my neck and my haircut was half finished. The barber was right behind me with a comb and a pair of scissors in his hands. The man who had been in the chair next to me was not so lucky. There
15 was shaving cream on one side of his face and his barber was running after him carrying a shaving brush in one hand and a razor in the other!

## Summary

Your answer must not be more than 83 words.

1.  Do you enjoy your visits to the barber shop or not?
2.  Do you learn a lot from your barber or not? Do you get your hair cut, or do you just sit and talk? *(not only . . . but also)*

3.  Did your talk last long last week or not?
4.  What did you hear? Did you stay in the shop, or did you all run outside? *(and so)*
5.  What did you have around your neck? What did another man have on his face? *(and)*
6.  What was your barber holding?
7.  What was the other barber holding?

The curving flight path of the Apollo 8 spacecraft would take astronauts Borman, Lovell and Anders behind the moon and out of touch with Earth. There they would fire the rocket engine to place them into a
5 lunar orbit. For decades men had dreamed of reaching the Moon, and of using it as a springboard to the stars. "One minute to *LOS* . . .," the voice from Houston said, marking the exact time before loss of signal. "All systems go. Safe journey, guys," the voice
10 continued. From the spacecraft, Anders answered for the crew, "Thanks a lot, troops. We'll see you on the other side." And then there was silence. LOS was complete. There were no voices, no telemetered data and no tracking. Ten minutes passed. The engine
15 should be firing now. Apollo 8 should be in lunar orbit. Twenty minutes dragged by, then thirty, thirty-five . . . "Go ahead, Houston. Apollo 8." Lovell's voice came through loud and clear, confirming lunar orbit.

**Summary**

Your answer must not be more than 85 words.

1.  Did the flight path of Apollo 8 take the astronauts to Mars or behind the Moon? Were they out of touch with Earth for just a few seconds or for more than half an hour? *(and)*
2.  Did they fire their rocket engine or not? Did they succeed in putting the spacecraft into lunar orbit,

or did they fail in their attempt? Could they report to Houston that everything was all right or not? *(and) (but)*

3. Did people on Earth know exactly what had happened, or did everybody wait anxiously for word from the spacecraft? *(Meanwhile, . . .)*

4. Were communications restored, or were they lost completely? Did Lovell's voice come through loud and clear, or was his voice weak and hard to understand? *(Finally, . . .) (and)*

5. Did he say, "We can't hear you, Houston," or did he say, "Go ahead, Houston"? Did people wonder what had happened, or did everybody know the mission was successful? *(and then)*

As soon as Mr. and Mrs. Graves moved into their charming old house in the country, they decided to remove all the faded green wallpaper from the walls. They began with the living room. Mr. Graves got a
5 ladder from the garage, while his wife got a bucket of water. Then they soaked the paper until it became soft. This way, they were able to scrape it off easily. After three hours of hard work, when they were both beginning to feel rather tired, Mr. Graves pulled away
10 a long strip of paper from over the fireplace. He called out excitedly to his wife. The former owner had written these words on the wall: "We hope you enjoy making this room look beautiful as much as we did. Don't work too hard. Take a break and have a cup of
15 coffee!" "What a good idea!" said Mrs. Graves, and she hurried into the kitchen.

**Summary**

Your answer must not be more than 75 words.

1. Did Mr. and Mrs. Graves move into a new house, or did they move into an old one?

2. What was on the walls? What did they decide to do? *(and)*
3. What did they do to the paper in the living room? Did it come off easily or not? *(and)*
4. How long did they work? How did they feel? *(and)*
5. Did Mr. Graves call to his wife just then or not?
6. Where had the former owner written the words "Take a break and have a cup of coffee"?
7. Did Mrs. Graves act on this suggestion or not?

Science has told us so much about the moon that it is fairly easy to imagine what it would be like to go there. It is certainly not a friendly place. Since there is no air or water, there can be no life of any kind. There
5 is not much variety of scenery either. For mile after mile there are only flat plains of dust with mountains around them. Above, the sun and stars shine in a black sky. If you step out of the mountain shadows, it means moving from severe cold into intense heat.
10 These extreme temperatures continually break rocks away from the surface of the mountains. The moon is also a very silent world, for sound waves can only travel through air. But beyond the broken horizon, you see a friendly sight. Our earth is shining more
15 brightly than the stars. From this distance, it looks like an immense blue, green and brown ball.

**Summary**

Your answer must not be more than 77 words.

1. Is the moon a friendly place, or is it an unfriendly place?
2. Is there any air or water there? Is there any life or not? Is there much variety of scenery or not? *(so ... neither ... nor)*
3. Do the sun and stars shine in a black sky, or do they shine in a blue sky? What effect do the temperature extremes have on the rocks? *(and)*

4.  Can sound waves travel on the moon or not? What is the effect of this? *(so)*
5.  How does the earth appear from there?

## 33

In the darkness, I leaned over the railing and watched the ship cutting a path through the waves. It was pleasant to be out on deck on such a beautiful night. But the captain had told me that the ship would
5 arrive at six o'clock in the morning. I therefore decided to return to my cabin because I wanted to get up early to take some pictures as the boat entered the harbor. It was very hot below, and in spite of my good intentions, I lay awake for hours listening to the ship's
10 engines. At last I went to sleep, but the noise of heavy chains and the sound of the ship's whistle woke me up. I dressed hurriedly, grabbed my camera and rushed up on deck. Then I had an unpleasant surprise. I was too late. The ship had already entered
15 the harbor and we were about to dock!

**Summary**

Your answer must not be more than 81 words.

1.  What time did they expect the ship to arrive in the harbor? Did the writer go to bed early or late? *(so)*
2.  What did he want to do in the morning?
3.  Was it hot in his cabin, or was it cold? Did it take him a long time to get to sleep or not? *(and)*
4.  Did the ship's whistle suddenly wake him up or not?
5.  Did he get dressed quickly, or did he take his time getting dressed? Did he hurry out on deck or not? Was it too early, or was it too late? *(and) (but)*
6.  Had the ship already come into the harbor or not? Were they moving along in the harbor or were they docking? *(and)*

**34**

A man driving along a lonely country road saw two men walking by the side of the road. One was on crutches and the other was carrying two suitcases. Since they were this far off the main road, it was 5 obvious that they were not hitchhikers but had simply run out of gas or had car trouble. Feeling sorry for them, he decided to offer them a ride. As he pulled over, however, the two men hurried off the road and disappeared into the bushes. They were in such a 10 hurry that the man carrying the suitcases left one of them behind. Since he had obviously frightened them, the driver got out and called to them to reassure them. Finally, he became suspicious and decided to open the suitcase. It was filled with jewelry, silverware and 15 other valuables. The police told him later that they were stolen goods which, by accident, he had helped to recover three hours after the robbery.

**Summary**

Your answer must not be more than 85 words.

1. Did a man driving on a country road see two men or not?
2. Was one of the men on crutches or on a bicycle? Was the other one carrying a box or two suitcases? Did the driver decide to give them a ride or not? *(and) (so)*

3. Did the driver speed up or pull over? Did the two men stop, or did they start running? Did they run on down the road, or did they disappear into the bushes? *(but) (and)*
4. Did they leave one of the suitcases lying beside the road, or did they take both of them with them? *(However, . . .)*
5. Did he take it to the police or not? Did he find out it contained stolen goods, or did he find out that it was worthless? *(and)*
6. Did they accuse him of stealing the suitcase, or did they congratulate him for finding the stolen items only three hours after the robbery?

Henry Ford was the first one to build cars which were fast, reliable and cheap. He was able to sell millions of them because he "mass-produced" them; that is, he made a great many cars of exactly the same
5 type. Henry Ford's father had hoped that his son would become a farmer, but the young man did not like the idea and went to Detroit where he worked as a mechanic. By the time he was twenty-nine, in 1892, he had built his first car. The first mass-produced car in
10 the world, the famous "Model T," appeared in 1908— five years after Henry had started his great Ford Motor Company. This car proved to be so popular that it remained unchanged for twenty years. Since Henry Ford's time, mass-production techniques have
15 become common in industry and have reduced the price of a great many products which otherwise would be very expensive.

**Summary**

Your answer must not be more than 78 words.

1. Did Henry Ford mass-produce cars, or did he make them by hand? Was he able to sell a great many of them, or did he sell only a few? *(so)*
2. What did Henry's father want him to be? Where did Henry go? What did he do instead? *(but) (and)*

3. Did he start the Ford Motor Company or not? When did he build the world's first mass-produced car? *(and)*
4. What did he call it?
5. Was the car very popular or not? How long did the model remain unchanged? *(so)*
6. Have mass-production methods been used in industry for just a few years, or have they been used ever since Henry Ford's time?

Since Mrs. Talbot had carefully locked the front door when she left the house, she was surprised to find it unlocked on her return. When she walked into the hallway, an extraordinary sight met her eyes. A
5 strange man was fast asleep on the sofa in the living room! Taking care not to disturb him, Mrs. Talbot left the house immediately. She went to a neighbor's house and called the police. She hastily explained what had happened and added that the man must
10 have picked the lock on the front door. The police arrived in a short while, and Mrs. Talbot returned to her house with two policemen. But it was obviously too late; the man had disappeared. Just then, to her surprise, her husband appeared at the head of the
15 stairs and greeted her. He explained that he had come home from the office early. Then he said, "I have a surprise for you. You've never met my cousin John from Michigan. He arrived this afternoon and I brought him home with me. He's going to spend a few
20 days with us."

**Summary**

Your answer must not be more than 85 words.

1. Had Mrs. Talbot locked the door when she left the house, or had she left the door open? Was she surprised to find it open or not? *(so)*
2. Was she relieved when she looked in the living room, or was she even more surprised?

3. Who was sleeping on the sofa?
4. Did she sit down in the living room, or did she leave immediately? Did she spend the afternoon at a neighbor's house, or did she come back a little later with two policemen? Was the man still there, or was he gone? *(and then) (but)*
5. Did her husband appear at the head of the stairs just then, or did he come to the front door just then?
6. Who did he say was visiting them? Did she still wonder who the strange man was, or did she realize the man on the sofa was her husband's cousin? *(and then)*

**37** "Now for the run home . . . I wonder if we can do it," wrote Captain Scott at the South Pole. The "run home" was a journey of 900 miles on which five men of great courage lost their lives. Fierce winds blew
5 against them across a desert of snow and ice, and they could walk only a few miles each day. A month later Evans died after a serious accident. Sometime later another member of the party, Captain Oates, could go no farther. One morning he said, "I am just
10 going outside and may be some time." He disappeared into the snow and never returned. Three men now struggled on until they were only eleven miles from their base camp where there was plenty of food. But a terrible snowstorm began and they had to
15 remain in their tent for days. A search party found their bodies a year later.

**Summary**

Your answer must not be more than 80 words.

1. How many miles was the return journey from the South Pole? Was the weather good or bad? Could Captain Scott and his four companions cover quite a few miles a day or only a few? *(but) (so)*
2. Which two men died on the way? *(Both . . . and)*

3. Did the other men give up, or did they keep going until they were only eleven miles from their base camp? Did they run into a rainstorm or a bad snowstorm? Did they have to stay in their tent for days or for just a few hours? *(but then) (and)*
4. What happened a year later?

Some people do not seem to have a mind of their own. They never express their own opinions and they do not make their own decisions. My brother is one of these people. Last night, for example, he was
5 planning to spend a quiet evening at home reading a book. At about seven-thirty, however, his friend Tom dropped by. "Let's watch TV tonight," Tom suggested. "Okay," my brother said. By ten o'clock my brother was tired and sleepy, and I am sure he
10 wanted to go to bed. But Tom was not tired. "Let's go out and get a hamburger," Tom said. "Good idea," my brother replied. He very often says things he does not mean and does things he really does not want to do. Worse than that, he does not say the things he would
15 like to say or do a lot of the things he would like to do.

**Summary**

Your answer must not be more than 82 words.

1. Does your brother seem to have a mind of his own or not?
2. How often does he express his own opinions? Does he make his own decisions or not? *(and)*
3. Did he plan to read a book last night or not? Did his friend Tom drop by or did he call him on the telephone? Did he suggest they read a book or watch TV? *(but) (and)*
4. Was your brother wide awake at ten o'clock, or was he ready to go to bed? Was Tom sleepy, or did he want to go out for a hamburger? Did your

brother go out with him, or did he stay home?
*(but) (so)*

5. Does your brother often do things he does not really want to do or not?

By noon, the small group of boy scouts led by their scoutmaster had reached a height of 2,500 feet. At this point the party had to stop climbing because one of the boys fell and broke his leg. The only thing the
5 scoutmaster could do was return to the mountain cabin where they had spent the night. From there, he telephoned the police. Since no rescue team could reach the boy quickly enough, the National Guard sent out a helicopter with a doctor on board. The
10 helicopter soon arrived on the scene, but the sides of the mountain were so steep that it could not land. However, the pilot lowered the helicopter slowly and carefully toward the steep side of the mountain near the spot where the boy was lying. With one of the
15 skids of the helicopter just inches from the ground, the pilot kept the helicopter hovering in midair while the scoutmaster and his helpers lifted the boy on board.

**Summary**

Your answer must not be more than 83 words.

1. How high had the scoutmaster and his group of scouts climbed?
2. What happened to one of the boys at this point? What did the scoutmaster do? *(so)*
3. What did he do from there? Did a helicopter quickly arrive on the scene or not? *(and)*
4. Was the mountain very steep or not? Could the pilot land or not? Did he give up, or did he keep the helicopter hovering near the ground? *(and) (so)*
5. What did the scouts do then?

**40** After crawling out the full length of the steel girder, the welder positioned himself as securely as he could and prepared to lower his face shield to begin the welding operation. As he raised his hand to the
5 helmet, he glanced down toward the ground twenty-two stories below, and all of a sudden he froze. The ground seemed to be moving, and for an instant he felt dizzy. Instinctively he pulled back and reached out to grasp the girder firmly with both hands. His hands
10 and arms were trembling and he was struggling to catch his breath. Slowly and cautiously, he leaned forward until his head was resting on the cold steel girder. In his ten years of experience on construction jobs, he had seen several men suddenly lose their
15 nerve for no apparent reason, but he never dreamed it could ever happen to him. With both arms wrapped tightly around the girder and with his legs locked together, he began to shout for help.

**Summary**

Your answer must not be more than 83 words.

1. Was a welder working on a structure four stories high or twenty-two stories high?
2. Had he crawled out on a girder or had he climbed up a ladder? Was he preparing to lower his face

shield or not? Could he weld a joint or not? *(and)* *(so that)*

3. Did he look up in the sky just then, or did he glance down at the ground? Did he move all of a sudden, or did he freeze? *(and)*

4. Were his hands and arms trembling, or were they steady? Was he having a hard time breathing, or was he breathing normally? *(and)*

5. Did he wrap his arms around the girder or not? Did he go to sleep, or did he begin to shout for help? *(and)*

6. Did he feel secure on the girder that high up, or did he realize he had suddenly lost his nerve?

# THE COMPLEX SENTENCE

## To the teacher

### 1. Aims

(a) To enable students to write complex sentences.

(b) To enable students to put these sentences together to form a continuous paragraph.

(c) To give students practice in writing continuous prose using conjunctions, adverbs, participles and connecting phrases.

(d) To provide additional exercises in writing simple and compound sentences (practiced in Sections 1 and 2).

(e) To guide students towards an elementary form of summary writing by providing them with specific information *(Main Points)* to be used in developing an orderly paragraph.

### 2. How the student should work

This section has been divided into two parts, each consisting of ten passages. In both parts the student will be required to write complex sentences in a logical sequence. The method for doing this, however, will differ in each section.

(a) **Question and Answer**  The question-answer technique used in Sections 1 and 2 will be used in the first part of this section (passages 41—50). In working with these first ten passages, students will be asked to write complex sentences by answering two or sometimes three questions with a single sentence. The conjunctions to be used are given in parentheses. The following is an example:

> Did he open the door or not? What did he find? What had accidentally entered the room? *(On opening) (that) (and that)*

The answer would be given as one complex sentence, as follows:

> *On opening* the door, he found *that* the window had been left open *and that* a bird had accidentally flown into the room.

(b) **Word Order** The student should be given to understand that each clause in a complex sentence usually keeps to the Subject/Verb/Complement and/ or Verb modifier pattern.

This is particularly obvious in indirect speech; for example:

| Subject | Verb | | | Complement | |
|---------|------|---------|------|------------|------------|
| | | *Subject* | | *Verb* | *Complement* |
| **He** | **said** | **that** | **he** | **would write** | **a letter.** |

When writing complex sentences, students often find it difficult to decide when to insert a subject and when to leave it out. Sometimes they employ one subject too many, as in the following:

> The man when he left the house he . . .
>
> Should be: When the man left the house, he . . .

Or again, the following:

> The people who live next door they asked me . . .
>
> Should be: The people who live next door asked me . . .

46

At other times, students may incorrectly omit the subject; for example:

> When the man left the house forgot to lock . . .

Should be: When the man left the house, he forgot to lock . . .

Special attention should be given to these difficulties.

### 3. Vocabulary range

The students' passive vocabulary should be about 1,600 words. The actual range (taking into account the words used in previous sections) is about 1,400 words. The passages have been graded in order of increasing difficulty.

### 4. Length of each passage

About 230 words (maximum of two paragraphs).

### 5. Length of summaries

Passages 41 to 50: 80 to 100 words
Passages 51 to 60: 80 words

### 6. Structures

All tenses, active and passive. A reasonable working knowledge of most elementary structures has been assumed. The students will be expected to join sentences using participles and prepositions + Verb-*ing* (e.g., after leaving, on hearing, etc.).

The conjunctions which the students will be expected to use in this section are as follows: *although/ though, because, even, if/whether, hardly . . . when, since, so that . . ., would, that* (indirect speech), *to/in order to, unless, until, when, where, which, while, who.*

Connecting words and phrases the students will be expected to use are the following: *some time later, just after, in time, that evening, at first, rather than, a little later, after a time, after this, at last, finally, only to* + verb, *just before, in spite of the fact that.*

## To the student

In this section, you will learn how to use conjunctions to form *complex* sentences, that is, sentences which contain one main idea and one or more less important ideas. The section has been divided into two parts. Separate instructions are given for each part. Before you begin the first part of the section, read these instructions very carefully:

### How to work

1. Read each passage carefully two or three times.
2. Write a full answer to each question. When several questions are given together, join your answers with the conjunctions or phrases given in parentheses. Each answer you write must be *a complete sentence.*
3. Your answers to the questions must follow each other in sequence, so that all your sentences will form *a complete paragraph.*
4. Read through your work and correct your mistakes.
5. Count the number of words in your paragraph. Do not go over the word limit. At the end of your paragraph, mark down the number of words you have used.
6. Give your paragraph a title.

Study this example carefully and then try to do passages 41 to 50 in the same way by yourself.

### Example

My neighbor's children love playing hide-and-seek as all children do, but no one imagined that a game they played last week would be reported in the local newspaper.

5     One afternoon, they were playing in the vacant lot down by the corner. Young Paul, who is only five years old, found the perfect place to hide. His sister, Natalie, had shut her eyes and was counting to ten when Paul noticed the storage mail box at the corner

10   and saw that the metal door was standing open. The mailman had just taken out several sacks of mail and had carried them to his truck which was standing at the curb a few feet away. Paul climbed into the storage box and pulled the door closed so hard that it

15   locked. Soon realizing what he had done, he became frightened and started crying. Meanwhile, Natalie was looking for him everywhere but could not find him. It was lucky that she happened to pause at the corner for a minute and heard her brother's cries. She imme-

20   diately ran to tell the mailman who hurried back from his truck to unlock the metal door. Paul was now free, but he had had such a bad scare that he could not stop crying. The mailman, however, soon found a way of making him laugh again. He told him that the next

25   time he wanted to hide in a mail box, he should remember to put a stamp on himself!

### Summary

Your answer must not be more than 85 words.

1. What were your neighbor's children playing in a vacant lot one afternoon?
2. Had the storage mail box been left open or not? Where did young Paul hide? Did he lock himself in or not? *(Finding that) (and)*
3. When did his sister, Natalie, realize where he was hiding? What did she do? *(so)*
4. How did the mailman make Paul stop crying after he let him out? *(After letting . . . by telling . . .)*

### Answer

*A Strange "Letter"*

   One afternoon, my neighbor's children were playing hide-and-seek in a vacant lot. *Finding that* the storage mail box had been left open, young Paul hid in it *and* locked himself in. His sister, Natalie, realized where he was hiding when she heard his cries, *so* she ran to tell the mailman. *After letting* him out, the mailman made Paul stop crying *by telling* him that the next time he wanted to hide in a mail box, he should remember to put a stamp on himself!

(85 Words)

**41** The bus to Westlake was about to leave and Mrs. Greely was giving last-minute instructions to her six-year-old boy. "Call me the minute you get to Grandpa's," she was saying. She wished now she had not
5  given in. It was a four-hour ride, and she was worried sick.

As the bus pulled away, Robby waved and then pretended he was a spy. His mission was to follow the man sitting next to him to a secret meeting. "How far
10  are you going?" the man asked. Robby told him he was going to his grandfather's farm; he didn't want to give away his mission! Robby and the man talked for a long time until the man said, "This is Hampton. I live here." It was a rest stop and everybody got off. Robby
15  kept out of sight and followed the man into the station. Robby watched the man approach a woman who was waiting by the door to the parking lot behind the bus station. Now Robby had all the information he needed, so he went back to the bus, but it was not
20  there. As the man who had been on the bus drove out of the parking lot, he was surprised to see Robby standing in front of the station crying. He told Robby the bus had gone, but he and his wife would drive him to the Westlake bus station. At nine o'clock Mrs.
25  Greely answered the phone and breathed a sigh of relief that Robby had arrived safely. "You see . . .?" the boy's grandfather said, and she agreed it had been silly of her to worry.

**Summary**

Your answer must not be more than 100 words.

1.  Did Mrs. Greely put Robby on a bus or a train going to Westlake?

2. Was he going to his aunt's house or his grand-father's house? Was it a two-hour or a four-hour bus ride? *(and)*
3. Was Robby ten, or was he only six? Was his mother worried sick or not? *(Since Robby ...)*
4. Who did Robby talk to on the bus?
5. Where did the bus make a stop? Did everybody get off for a few minutes or not? *(and)*
6. Did Robby get back on the bus, or did he miss the bus in Hampton? Did a man and his wife drive him to Westlake in their car or not? *(but)*
7. Would Mrs. Greely have been even more worried if she had known that Robby missed the bus in Hampton? *(If Mrs. Greely ...)*

It was years since I had visited my hometown and I was determined to enjoy my stay. I went to see my old friend Tom Clark who, along with his other responsi-bilities, was vice president of the civic association. At
5 the time, Tom was busy making final arrangements for a distinguished writer to give a talk on modern literature at the public library. Since this was a subject that interested me, I gladly accepted Tom's invitation to go with him.
10 Tom was going to introduce the guest speaker that evening, so we went to the library a little bit early to greet him. Since he had not yet arrived, I left Tom and went into the main Reading Room where a large audience had already gathered. I was disappointed to
15 find that I did not know a single person there. Just before the talk was due to begin, I saw Tom motioning to me from the doorway. He looked worried about something, so I got up immediately and went back to see him. He explained that he had just had a
20 telephone call from the writer's secretary. Our guest speaker had missed his flight and would not be arriving! While we were thinking about the problem, Tom suddenly asked me if I would mind filling in as speaker. I hardly had time to think about the matter

25　when suddenly I found I was being led back into the Reading Room to address the waiting audience!

## Summary

Your answer must not be more than 87 words.

1. What old friend did you go to see when you returned to your hometown after many years' absence? *(On returning . . .)*
2. Had Tom invited a famous artist or a distinguished writer to give a talk at the city library?
3. Did the subject interest you or not? Did he ask you to go with him or not? *(Since the subject . . .)*
4. Who telephoned that evening just before the talk began? Was the speaker going to be able to be there or not? *(That evening . . . to say that)*
5. Did Tom then suggest that you should address the audience or not? Where did he take you? *(and)*

A man in Port Orchard by the name of Henry has a most unusual hobby. He likes planting flowers in strange places. When spring comes around, you can always tell that Henry has been busy because the dirty
5　sides of rivers, the banks along railroad tracks and land covered with trash suddenly come alive with flowers of all kinds. In his spare time, with pockets full of seeds, Henry goes riding around on his bicycle. He

carries a long reed with him to blow seeds into spots
10 that are hard to reach. When his flowers die, he goes
around again to collect the seeds. In this way, he
always has an ample supply.

Many people make fun of Henry, but he never
seems to let it bother him. Recently, I was having
15 coffee with him and he told me that once he was
planting seeds in a large vacant lot when the owner
came along and sent him away. Henry returned some
days later when there was no one around. You can
imagine how surprised the owner was one day several
20 months later when he saw a large letter "H" in flowers
covering the entire lot! Henry took me to his house
one time, and I was astonished to see that there was
only one small flowerpot in the house. When I
questioned him about this, he answered, "They're not
25 real. They're artificial. Real flowers should be out
there where they belong." And he pointed out the
window to his large flower garden.

### Summary

Your answer must not be more than 72 words.

1.  What is Henry's hobby?
2.  Does he ride around on a bicycle in his spare time,
    or does he go around on foot? Why does he take a
    long reed with him? *(and)*
3.  Do people sometimes make fun of him or not?
    Can they ever keep him from planting seeds on
    unused pieces of property? *(but)*
4.  Does Henry have real flowers in his own house, or
    does he have artificial ones? What does he be-
    lieve? *(Even though he loves flowers so much, . . .
    because)*

 The whole family objected violently when I said that
I was going to Europe over the Christmas holidays
with a college friend of mine. Mother said that since
there was going to be a family reunion, I really ought

5 to stay at home. Although I always enjoyed these
occasions, nothing could persuade me to change my
mind.

A week before Christmas, my friend and I flew to
Madrid and then traveled by train through Spain,
10 France and Germany. On Christmas Eve we arrived in
a small town in southern Germany and were amazed
to find so much activity in the town. The streets were
crowded with people, and the shops were full of all
kinds of interesting things. We walked around for
15 hours and then just before midnight we went to listen
to Christmas carols sung by children around the
brightly lit tree in the main square. We returned to our
hotel late that night, looking forward to the next day
when we planned to have Christmas dinner at the best
20 restaurant in town. However, in the morning the
streets were deserted. To make matters worse, everything was closed up tight—even the restaurants. We
searched in vain for hours and finally had to return to
our hotel feeling unhappy and lonely. Our Christmas
25 "feast" was a sack of fruit which my friend happened
to buy the day before. Our thoughts sadly turned to
home where, at that moment, our families must have
been wishing us a "Merry Christmas."

**Summary**

Your answer must not be more than 95 words.

1. Did your family want you to stay home for Christmas or not? Where did you go? Who did you go
   with? *(In spite of the fact that . . .)*
2. Where were you on Christmas Eve?
3. Where did you go that night? Why? *(Just before
   midnight . . . to . . .)*
4. Where did you intend to eat the next day? Did you
   search for hours or not? Did you find everything
   closed or open? What did you do? *(but after
   searching . . . so . . .)*
5. What did you eat? How did you feel when you
   thought of your families? *(and)*

As it came near the corner, the taxi stopped
suddenly. The driver got out looking very puzzled. A
big truck which had been following the taxi stopped
too. The taxi driver was now standing at the corner
5 looking up at the sky and the truck driver got out and
joined him. A number of cars behind them were
forced to stop as well and soon a large crowd of
people had gathered at the corner.

The cause of all this trouble was a very strange
10 noise. It sounded as if thousands and thousands of
birds were chirping. The sound of so many birds
together was quite unnerving and many people
looked frightened. The most extraordinary thing was
that, apart from one or two pigeons, there was not a
15 bird in sight. No one was able to solve the mystery—
until two traffic patrolmen arrived on the scene. They
walked all around the area for a while and then
stopped over near the railroad tracks beside a
billboard advertisement for a movie. Since the noise
20 seemed to be coming from around there, they
climbed up and found that two loudspeakers had
been hidden behind the advertisement. The bird
noises were being broadcast to attract attention to the
movie advertisement. The advertising company was
25 ordered to remove the loudspeakers, on the grounds
that they were a public nuisance and that they created
a serious traffic hazard.

### Summary

Your answer must not be more than 81 words.

1. Where did a large crowd gather after the traffic
   stopped?
2. Did everyone look puzzled or not? Could they
   hear thousands of birds or not? Were there many
   in sight? (because . . . although there were hardly
   any)
3. Who arrived on the scene? Did they trace the
   noise to an old railroad station or to a billboard?
   (Then . . . and)

4.  Did they climb up on the billboard or not? Where was the noise coming from? Where were they hidden? *(After climbing . . . they found that . . . which . . .)*
5.  What did the advertising company have to do? Was it a poor advertisement for the movie or was it a public nuisance? *(because)*

Dark black clouds in the sky meant one thing and one thing only: there was going to be a thunderstorm. Not one of us had brought an umbrella, or even a raincoat, so when Jack suggested that we go into the
5 nearby museum, we all agreed immediately. Since we had been shopping all morning and were now feeling very tired, it would be a pleasure to sit down. We arrived at the entrance to the museum just as large drops of rain were beginning to fall.
10 The museum was completely deserted and very peaceful. We sat down in the main hall and listened to the rain beating against the windows. Suddenly there was a big commotion out in the entry hall. Then a large group of schoolchildren came in, led by two
15 teachers. The poor teachers were trying to keep them quiet and get them to behave, but they did not pay the slightest attention. The children ran here and there like wild animals. Apologizing for this lack of discipline, the teachers explained that the children
20 were too excited to settle down. Eventually the noise proved too much for us and we decided to leave. As Jack remarked when we were back outside walking in the rain, the children had more right to be in the museum than we did. After all, they had come on an
25 educational visit, while we had simply wanted to get in out of the rain.

**Summary**

Your answer must not be more than 84 words.

1.  Was there going to be a thunderstorm or not? Did you have umbrellas and raincoats with you?

Where did you decide to go? *(and since)*
2. When did it begin raining?
3. Was it very quiet in the main hall or not? Who came in? *(At first . . . until . . .)*
4. Who was in charge of them? Could they keep them in order or not? *(but)*
5. What did you prefer to do rather than put up with so much noise? *(Rather than . . .)*

**47** Old Sally Gibbs was a very strange woman. The beautiful house she lived in was surrounded by trees and lovely flower gardens. But she hardly ever went out. Although a housekeeper looked after her, her
5 only real companions were two cats. For years she had refused to see any of her relatives because she felt that all they were interested in was her money.

She was right about that. After her death, all of her relatives gathered at the house to hear Sally's lawyer
10 read her will. They were all sure that Sally had left a fortune and they each wanted a share. This led to violent arguments. In particular, they quarreled about the house. Sally's nephew felt that it should go to him since he was the only one who used to visit his old
15 aunt before she cut herself off from the family. Sally's cousin objected to this, and soon there was a heated argument in the living room while they waited for the lawyer to arrive. When the lawyer got there, the nephew said jokingly that he supposed his aunt had

20 left a big pile of debts. The lawyer did not even smile
at this and asked them all to sit down. He began to
read the will in a solemn voice. Sally had been
immensely rich—but she had left every penny of her
fortune to her two cats!

**Summary**

Your answer must not be more than 80 words.

1. Did Sally Gibbs want to see any of her relatives or
   not? Did she prefer to live with members of her
   family, or did she prefer to live alone with her two
   cats? *(preferring)*
2. Why did Sally's relatives come to her house after
   her death?
3. Did they think she had left them a great deal of
   money or not? Did they quarrel violently among
   themselves just before the lawyer arrived at the
   house or not? *(Thinking that...)*
4. What did they discover when the will was read?
   *(However)*

An old friend from California, who was going to
spend a few days with me, called from the airport to
tell me that he had arrived. I was not able to leave the
office, but I had made plans for his arrival. After
5 explaining where my new house was, I told him that I
had left the key under the doormat. Since I knew it
would be pretty late before I could get home, I
suggested that he make himself at home and help
himself to anything that was in the refrigerator.
10 Two hours later my friend phoned me from the
house. At the moment, he said, he was listening to
some of my records after having had a delicious meal.
He had found the skillet and fried two eggs, and had
helped himself to some cold chicken in the refrigera-
15 tor. Now, he said, he was drinking a glass of orange

juice and he hoped I would join him soon. When I asked him if he had had any difficulty finding the house, he answered that the only problem was that he had not been able to find the key under the doormat,

20 but fortunately, the living room window by the apple tree had been left open and he had climbed in through the window. I listened to all this in astonishment. There is no apple tree outside my window, but there is one by the living room window of my next-

25 door neighbor's house!

**Summary**

Your answer must not be more than 90 words.

1. Where were you when your friend arrived from California? Did you tell him how to get to your house or not? *(so)*
2. Where did you tell him the key was? Did you suggest that he make himself at home or not? *(and)*
3. Who phoned some time later? Had he had a delicious meal or not? *(... to say that ...)*
4. Was the key under the doormat or not? Had he climbed in through the living room window by the apple tree, or had he gone in through the kitchen door? *(Since the key ...)*
5. How did you feel when you heard this? Whose house had your friend accidentally entered? *(because)*

 It had been a tiring day and I was looking forward to a quiet evening. My husband would not be back until late and I had decided to settle down in a comfortable chair in the living room and read a good book. I put

5 the children to bed early and fixed a sandwich and a

cup of coffee. Soon I was settled comfortably with my book in front of me and the sandwich and cup of coffee on a tray beside me.

I was just beginning to eat when the telephone
10 rang. I dropped my book and hurried to answer it. By the time I got back to the living room, my coffee was cold. I ate the sandwich and began sipping cold coffee with the book still open to the first page. Suddenly there was a loud knock at the front door. It
15 startled me so much that I spilled some coffee on my skirt. The man at the door was looking for a certain address and wanted me to give him directions. It took me a long time to get rid of him. After that, I sat down again and managed to read a whole page without
20 further interruption—until the baby woke up. He started screaming at the top of his lungs so I rushed upstairs. He was still awake at 11 o'clock when my husband came home. I could have thrown something at him when he asked me if I had spent a pleasant
25 evening!

**Summary**

Your answer must not be more than 98 words.

1. What did the writer fix after she put the children to bed? *(After putting . . .)*
2. Was her husband going to be home early or late? How did she intend to spend the evening? *(Since her husband . . .)*
3. What happened just as she was beginning to eat?
4. Did she have time to sit down again or not? Who knocked at the door? *(She had hardly . . . when . . .)*
5. Did she begin reading when he left or not? Why did she have to stop? *(but . . . because . . .)*
6. What did her husband ask her when he got home at 11 o'clock? Was she happy, or did she feel like throwing something at him? *(On returning . . . and . . .)*

The elderly woman behind the wheel now regretted that she had stopped to pick up the two young hitch-hikers. As they hurriedly loaded their backpacks into the car, the young man turned and shouted, "Come
5 on, Sam!" Almost immediately a huge, long-haired dog that had been lying beside the road got up, shook himself violently, and then came lumbering toward the car. Two other dogs, a beagle and a mangy-looking cocker spaniel, followed a few feet
10 behind. The woman gasped when she saw the monstrous animals approaching. She wondered why she had not noticed the dogs when she first caught sight of the young couple thumbing a ride. There was nothing she could do about it now, she told herself.
15 She certainly could not bring herself to tell them that the dogs could not ride in her car. Instead she forced a polite smile and asked, "Is there going to be enough room for you in the back seat?" That was a mistake, as she quickly realized, and she was sorry that she
20 had brought the subject up. "It's going to be a little crowded," the young girl said, "but Sam can ride in the front seat with you if that's all right."

As they started off, both dogs in the back seat were barking and clawing at the windows. The woman
25 glanced nervously at Sam who by this time was sprawled out comfortably on the seat beside her,

panting loudly. Then and there she made a secret vow to herself about hitchhikers.

## Summary

Your answer must not be more than 97 words.

1. What did a woman see on the highway? Did she have plenty of room or not? What did she decide to do? *(Driving . . . and since . . .)*
2. Did the hitchhikers load their backpacks into the car, or did they leave them by the side of the road? Did they call to their dogs or not? Were the dogs hiding under the car, or were they sleeping nearby? *(After loading . . . that were . . .)*
3. Did the woman find out they were traveling alone or that they had three dogs with them? Was she glad she had decided to give them a ride, or was she sorry she had stopped? Was it too late or not? *(When . . . but . . .)*
4. Were two of the dogs put in the back seat or not? Was there plenty of room, or was it crowded? Did the big dog have to ride in front, or was there enough room in the back seat for all three dogs? *(but since)*
5. Did the woman park the car, or did she drive off? Did the woman vow to herself that next time she would drive a bigger car or that she would never stop for hitchhikers again? *(vowing)*

## To the teacher

### How the student should work

In the remaining part of this section, the student will be asked to work in a slightly different way. The "question-answer" technique will no longer be used. Instead, the student will be given a set of notes to use in writing sentences. As before, the student will be given conjunctions and connecting phrases needed to form complex sentences and to develop a paragraph summary. In writing the summary, the student may of course refer directly to the reading passage.

## To the student

The assignments that follow are slightly different from those you have done so far. There are no questions to answer in these exercises; the "questions" have already been answered for you in note form *(Main Points)*. You will be asked to use the notes in writing sentences and then (using the connecting words given) to join the sentences together in the form of a paragraph.

Before you begin reading passages 51 to 60, read these instructions very carefully:

### How to work

1.   Read each passage carefully two or three times.
2.   Read the instructions given after each reading passage. Below the instructions you will find a list of *Main Points* along with a list of *Connectors.* Using the conjunctions and phrases given under *Connectors* and the notes given under *Main Points,* write complete sentences and join them to form a paragraph summary of the reading.
3.   Read through your work and correct any mistakes you may have made.
4.   Count the number of words in your paragraph. Do not go over the word limit. At the end of your paragraph, indicate the number of words you have used.
5.   Give your paragraph a title.

Study this example carefully, then try to do passages 51 to 60 in the same way by yourself.

### Example

Forty-two horses had taken their positions on the starting line for the biggest race of the season. The track had many obstacles and was extremely difficult

and dangerous, so few horses were expected to finish
5  the race. All eyes were on the favorites, College Boy
and Sweet Seventeen. Both horses had won many
races in the past and seemed to have equal chances
of winning today.

Although most of the horses got off to a good start,
10  it was not long before more than half of them were out
of the race. As was expected, College Boy and Sweet
Seventeen had moved out in front, with the remaining
horses grouped together some distance behind them.
On one of the dangerous turns, three of the horses
15  leading the group stumbled and fell, creating an
additional obstacle for the riders following close
behind them. As the race progressed, there were
more and more horses moving around the track
without riders. Towards the end, there were only three
20  horses left in the race. College Boy and Sweet
Seventeen were still leading, and a completely
unknown horse, Tom Thumb, was trailing way behind
them. The crowd was very disappointed when the
riders of the two favorites were thrown from their
25  horses on the last jump, but everyone roared with
delight when College Boy continued on his own and
"won" the race—without a rider. Tom Thumb now
was taking his time and the crowd cheered and
applauded as he crossed the finish line without a rival
30  in sight.

### Instructions

In not more than 80 words, describe what happened
from the moment the horses started off until the end
of the race.

| Main Points | Connectors |
|---|---|
| 1. Race began. ⎤ | As soon as |
| 2. Favorites, C. Boy, S. Seventeen ⎟ | |
|    ahead. ⎦ | |
| 3. A turn—riders thrown off. ⎤ | On |
| 4. Horses following—out of race. ⎦ | and |
| 5. Three left: favorites, unknown. ⎤ | Towards the end |

6. Riders fell off.           ⎤ *However*
7. C. Boy "won"—by himself. ⎦ *though*
8. T. Thumb alone—real winner. ⎦ *Since*

**Answer**

### An Exciting Race

*As soon as* the race began, the favorites, College Boy and Sweet Seventeen, moved ahead. *On* a dangerous turn a few riders were thrown off *and* most of the horses following dropped out of the race. *Towards the end,* there were only three left—the favorites and an unknown horse, Tom Thumb. *However,* the riders of both favorites fell off too, *though* College Boy continued by himself and "won." *Since* Tom Thumb was now alone, he became the real winner.

(80 Words)

As the small twin-engine plane passed over the airport, everyone aboard sensed that something was wrong. The plane was bouncing around violently, and although the passengers had fastened their seat belts,
5  they did not feel very secure. At that moment, the door to the pilot's compartment swung open, and the passenger nearest the door stared into the cockpit in disbelief. The pilot was slumped over in his seat and his right arm was dangling loosely at his side.
10    Turning to the other five passengers and speaking quickly but almost in a whisper, he informed them that something had happened to the pilot and asked if anybody knew anything about flying a plane. No one replied, but after a moment's hesitation, a young boy
15  sitting at the back got up and came forward. The passenger by the door helped the boy move the pilot's body aside, and then the boy slid into the pilot's seat. He listened to instructions from the airport control tower and talked back and forth with the controller.
20  The boy circled the airport several times, following instructions from the tower on how to move the

controls. However, the danger had not yet passed.
The terrible moment came when he had to begin the
landing. Guiding the plane toward the runway, he
25  lowered it closer and closer to the ground. As it
touched down, the plane shook violently and then zig-
zagged down the long runway until finally it came to a
stop. Outside, rescue teams who had been waiting
anxiously, rushed toward the plane to congratulate
30  the thirteen-year-old "pilot" on his successful landing.

### Instructions

In not more than 80 words, describe what happened
after the boy went up to the pilot's compartment.

| Main Points | | Connectors |
|---|---|---|
| 1. Moved pilot, boy sat down. | ⎤ | *After moving* . . . |
| 2. Listened instructions—<br>   radio—control tower. | ⎦ | *and* |
| 3. Boy—back and forth—<br>   controller. | ⎤⎦ | |
| 4. Circled airport several times. | ⎤ | *Then* |
| 5. Instructions—controller—<br>   move controls. | ⎦ | *following* . . .<br>*how to* . . . |
| 6. Touched down, shook violently. | ⎤ | *On* . . . |
| 7. Zig-zag—runway, stopped<br>   safely. | ⎦ | *then* . . .<br>*until* . . . |
| 8. Rescue teams rushed—<br>   congratulate "pilot"—landing. | ⎤⎦ | *After this* . . .<br>*to* . . . |

The tour guide had warned us that the Palace
Hotel was a very old building without any modern
conveniences. Since we had been staying in modern
hotels, we did not look forward to our scheduled four-
5  day visit. As it turned out, however, we all thoroughly
enjoyed the experience. The ancient brick walls of the
hotel are covered with plaster and supported by heavy
wooden beams. All of the windows are made up of

small squares of glass held together by thin strips of
10 lead. The hotel owner is a cheerful fellow who loves
collecting strange ornaments and the hotel is like a
museum inside.

There had been a new addition just a few weeks
before our visit. The owner had bought a very curious
15 object: an elaborate clock with plaster figures of
people and animals. This clock, which became the
highlight of our visit, can best be described as a
gigantic music box. It is over 15 feet long with a
complete farm scene which comes to life every hour.
20 As the clock begins to strike the hour with an
assortment of bells and chimes, the people and
animals begin to move and make noises. Chickens
cluck, roosters crow, cows moo and pigs grunt. This
amazing performance continues for ten minutes every
25 hour. Although we enjoyed the clock, the one
drawback was that two people were needed to turn
the big crank to wind it up for each performance. By
developing an hourly winding schedule, we arranged
it so that no one had to be "on duty" more than twice
30 a day, but by the end of our visit everyone agreed that
the owner's next addition should be an electric motor.

### Instructions

Make a summary of the passage from line 10 (The
hotel owner . . .) to the end in not more than 90 words.

| Main Points | Connectors |
|---|---|
| 1. Palace Hotel owner—large collection strange objects. | *who*<br>*recently . . .*<br>*which . . .* |
| 2. Bought "clock"—figures, people, animals. | |
| 3. Like gigantic music box. | *Over fifteen feet long, . . .* |
| 4. Clock strikes—figures move, make noises. | *When* |
| 5. Performance goes on— 10 minutes. | *and* |

6. Drawback—two people needed—crank.    ] However . . . / to . . .

7. Developed schedule—nobody—more than two times.    ] This meant that . . . so that . . .

8. Left the hotel—all agreed—owner needs—electric motor—operate "clock."    ] On leaving . . . / to . . .

## 53

We were about to gather up our picnic things and return to our car when a man appeared. He looked very annoyed and asked us angrily if we realized that we were on private property. My father looked very
5  confused, and the man then pointed to a sign which said that picnicking and camping were strictly forbidden. Poor father explained that he had not seen the sign and did not realize that it was private property. Although my father apologized, the man did not seem
10  satisfied and asked him for his name and address. All the way home, we were so upset that hardly anyone said a word. This unpleasant experience had spoiled a wonderful day in the country.

All during that week, we wondered what would
15  happen. We stayed at home the following Sunday, even though it was a beautiful day. About noon, a big limousine pulled up in front of our house. We were astonished when we saw several people getting ready to have a picnic in our front yard. My father got very
20  angry and went out to ask them what they thought they were doing. You can imagine his surprise when he recognized the man who had taken down our name and address the week before! Both men burst out laughing, and my father welcomed the strangers
25  into our house. Eventually, we became good friends—but all of us learned a lesson we have never forgotten.

**Instructions**

In not more than 80 words, describe what happened after the man pointed out that picnicking was forbidden.

| **Main Points** | **Connectors** |
|---|---|
| 1. My father explained— private property. | Although . . . that . . . |
| 2. Man not satisfied, took name and address. | and |
| 3. Went home—upset. | We all |
| 4. Following Sunday—noon. | |
| 5. Limousine—in front. | |
| 6. Several people—picnic—yard. | and |
| 7. Father angry—laughed— recognized. | but . . . when . . . who . . . |
| 8. Week before—invited strangers—house. | and . . . |

**54**

Martin Thompson's funeral was a quiet affair. It was attended by the only relatives he had in the world, his niece and nephew, and by a few friends. Marty had led a hard life looking for gold in a remote part of Alaska.
5 He often declared that one day he would find a nugget of gold as big as his head and then retire and live in comfort the rest of his life, but his dreams of great wealth never came true. However, a curious thing happened to him in the last weeks of his life, and
10 although no one knew it, Marty died a contented man.

He was digging post holes one day when his shovel struck something hard. Finding a large stone, he got down on his hands and knees and managed to

unearth it. It shone curiously in the sunlight. As he
15 stared at the stone, it dawned on him what it was—a
large gold nugget! Tears streamed down his face as
he realized that his lifelong dream had come true. Still
on the ground, he sat motionless for a few minutes. It
was as though a great burden had been lifted from
20 him. Breathing a deep sigh, he deposited the nugget
back in the ground and covered up the hole. With the
shovel over his shoulder and grinning broadly, he
walked back to his cabin.

### Instructions

Write a summary of the passage from line 3
(Marty . . .) to the end in not more than 80 words.

| Main Points | Connectors |
|---|---|
| 1. Worked on his own—<br>gold digger—Alaska. | *Martin Thompson*<br>*had . . .* |
| 2. Sure he would find a lot of<br>gold. | *Though* |
| 3. Dreams of wealth—<br>lived in poverty. | *and* |
| 4. Curious thing. | *However, . . .* |
| 5. No one knew—contented man. | *although . . . and* |
| 6. Dig—shovel, something hard. | *He . . . when* |
| 7. Look at stone—realize—<br>large nugget. | *When* |
| 8. Tears—realize—dream true. | *and . . . because* |
| 9. Realize—not really interested<br>—great wealth. | *Also, . . .* |
| 10. Satisfaction—find nugget. | *but only* |

We were losing the battle. Our King was old and
weak and could hardly move. He was hiding just outside the castle walls. Of the three soldiers who had
been appointed to protect him, two had been killed
5 while on duty, and I was left alone.

From where I was standing, I had a good view of the
battle. Fortunately for us, our Queen was young and
active. Tall, dark, and very beautiful, she looked
splendid out there on the battlefield with her knights
10 at her side. She had fought with great courage and
had already destroyed two enemy officers herself.
Since we had lost so many men, it was difficult for her
to attack. She therefore decided to do all she could to
defend the King. I was shocked when I saw a lowly
15 enemy soldier threatening her! He came up very
close, but her brave knights sacrificed themselves to
save her. Alone now, she was trapped by the enemy,
and although she fought hard, she too lost her life.
Great numbers of enemy officers and soldiers now
20 descended upon us and soon destroyed the castle.
Completely defeated, the King and I tried to run away
together, but it was too late. As the King moved up
behind me, I heard someone shout, "Checkmate!"
The chess game was over.

### Instructions

In not more than 80 words, write a summary of the
battle from the point of view of an observer (use third-
person forms).

| Main Points | Connectors |
|---|---|
| 1. King hiding—castle. | |
| 2. One soldier—defend him. | with |
| 3. Queen—fought bravely. | Meanwhile |
| 4. Two enemy officers. | and |
| 5. Soldier threatened. | When |
| 6. Knights gave up lives— Queen's life. | |
| 7. Queen—trapped—fought hard—killed. | Now alone . . . and although |
| 8. Enemy attacked— destroyed castle. | After this . . . and |
| 9. Soldier and King escape. | While |
| 10. Shouted. Game of chess. | thus ending |

## 56

It was very hot in the small courtroom and everybody was feeling sleepy. After a tiring morning, the clerks were anxious to get off for lunch, and even the judge must have felt relieved when the last case came
5 up before the court. A short, middle-aged man with gray hair and small blue eyes was now standing before him. The man had a peculiar look on his face and he kept looking around the courtroom as if he was trying very hard to figure out what was going on.
10 The man was accused of breaking into a house and stealing an inexpensive wristwatch. The witness who was called did not give a very clear account of what had happened. He claimed to have seen a man outside the house that night, but on being questioned
15 further, he confessed that he was not sure whether this was the man or not. The judge considered the matter for a short time and then declared that since there was no real proof, the man could not be found guilty of any crime. He said that the case was
20 dismissed and then rose to go. Meanwhile, the defendant looked very puzzled. It was clear from the expression on his face that he had not understood a thing. Noticing this, the judge paused for a moment and then the man looked at the judge and said,
25 "Excuse me, your honor, but do I have to give the watch back or not?"

### Instructions

Write a summary of the passage from line 5 (A short . . .) to the end in not more than 80 words.

| Main Points | Connectors |
|---|---|
| 1. Standing before judge. | ⎤ who |
| 2. Kept looking around courtroom. | ⎦ |
| 3. Accused—watch. | ⎤ He |
| 4. Witness not sure—really thief. | ⎦ but |
| 5. Clear proof. | ⎤ In the absence |
| 6. Dismissed case. | ⎦ |

72

7. Judge preparing to leave. ⎤ *While*
8. Not understood.         ⎟ *who*
9. Asked—return watch?     ⎦ *whether*

**57**

People are very careless with money. One occasionally hears that pet dogs or even small children have eaten dollar bills. Goats are supposed to be particularly fond of them. Many people have lost
5  their homes in fires which have also destroyed precious bundles of money hidden in mattresses. In this regard, banks are a great blessing because people no longer have to hide money in places where it can easily be destroyed or stolen. However,
10  accidents still happen—as I found out to my regret recently.

I gave my wife an old pair of jeans to wash and went out to work in the yard. My wife usually goes through my pockets before washing anything, but for some
15  reason she did not think of it this particular time. As I was raking leaves in the front yard, I suddenly remembered that there was a fifty-dollar money order in one of the pockets of the pants I had given her to wash. I dropped my rake and rushed into the house.
20  But it was too late. My wife told me that my pants had been in the washing machine for ten minutes already! I stopped the machine and pulled them out as quickly as I could. I nearly tore off the pockets as I frantically searched for the money order. Finally, I managed to
25  find the soggy bits of paper which had once been a fifty-dollar money order. To my great disappointment, I discovered that all of them were bleached pure white!

**Instructions**

In not more than 80 words, describe what happened from the moment the writer gave his pants to his wife to be washed.

| **Main Points** | **Connectors** |
|---|---|
| 1. Gave old jeans—to wash. | ⎤ *The writer* |
| 2. Went out, work in yard. | ⎦ *and* |
| 3. Remembered money order— pocket. | ⎤ *After a time . . .* ⎦ *which* |
| 4. Rushed inside. | ⎤ *He* |
| 5. Washing machine—already 10 minutes. | ⎦ *only to learn . . .* |
| 6. Stopped machine. | ⎤ *Then* |
| 7. Pulled pants out. | ⎥ |
| 8. Searched. | ⎦ *and* |
| 9. Found bits—bleached white. | ⎤ *Finally . . . which* |

The conductor went through car after car inquiring whether there was a doctor on the train. He found one at last and quickly led him to the dining car where a man was stretched out on the floor. The conductor
5 explained that he had discovered the man in the passageway between cars and had dragged him inside. The doctor loosened the man's collar and after examining him for a few minutes, told the conductor that the man would have to be taken to a hospital
10 immediately. When he heard this, the conductor answered that the nearest station was over seventy miles away and that it would take them more than an hour to get there. The doctor said timing was critical and suggested sending an urgent message to have an
15 ambulance waiting at the station. Meanwhile the man's condition was getting gradually worse.

There seemed to be no way of getting the man to a hospital in time until the conductor returned with the news that a helicopter was being sent out to meet the
20 train. Barely twenty minutes later, the helicopter appeared overhead. Shortly afterwards, the train was stopped and the man was carried off the train on a stretcher. The transfer was made in a matter of minutes, and before the train began to move again,
25 the helicopter was on its way to the hospital.

## Instructions

Describe what happened after the conductor explained how he had dragged the sick man into the dining car. Do not use more than 80 words.

| Main Points | Connectors |
|---|---|
| 1. Loosen collar—examine. | ] *After loosening . . .* |
| 2. Seriously ill—hospital. | ] *He realized . . .* <br> ] *and . . .* |
| 3. Train—seventy miles— nearest station. | ] *However* |
| 4. Conductor said—an hour— get there. | ] *. . . and . . .* |
| 5. Doctor's suggestion— conductor contacted, next station. | ] *Following* |
| 6. Returned—news— helicopter—meet train. | ] *and* |
| 7. Twenty minutes— helicopter—train stopped. | ] *. . . and . . .* |
| 8. Man—transfer—helicopter. | ] *A few minutes later* |
| 9. Helicopter—take off, for hospital. | ] *and* |

On my last day in Grants Pass, I decided to visit Wildlife Safari, an animal preserve near Roseburg. Leaving my hotel, I found my way to Interstate High-

way 5 and headed north. After entering the preserve
5 area, I stopped from time to time to take photographs
of different animals. A little later, I was delighted when
I saw a sign saying: "Caution: Lions. Stay in Your
Car." I had no intention of getting out, of course. I had
been driving through a wooded area and just then
10 came to a shallow stream. I started driving across the
stream and was about halfway when the rear wheels
began to spin; the car was stuck in the mud!

Complaining about my bad luck, I looked around
very carefully. There was not a lion in sight. I was soon
15 in the stream getting completely soaked, but there
was nothing I could do about moving the car. My first
impulse was to leave the car and start walking, but I
did not relish the idea of starting out on foot through
the woods. Remembering the warning about the
20 lions, I got back into the car for safety. I felt miserable
and I wondered how long it would be before I was
discovered by wild beasts. I could imagine elephants
charging at me, or lions deciding that I would make a
tasty meal! I was greatly relieved when, about two
25 hours later, an attendant drove up in a jeep and soon
hauled my car out of the stream. It took me some time
to recover from this experience, and I decided after
that to confine my visits to zoos.

**Instructions**

In not more than 80 words, give an account of the
writer's experiences while he was in the wildlife preserve area.

| **Main Points** | **Connectors** |
|---|---|
| 1. Took pictures—animals. | *After having . . .* |
| 2. Saw sign—lions. | *the writer . . . which* |
| 3. Drive across—stream. | *While* |
| 4. Car stuck. | |
| 5. Looked around—no lions—got out. | *He . . . and* *since . . .* |
| 6. Clothes—not move car. | *His . . . but . . .* |

7. Got back in, waited hours. ⎤ *Finally ... and ...*
8. Attendant arrived—jeep.  | *until*
9. Car pulled out. ⎦ *and*

Some time ago, scientists began experiments to find out whether it would be possible to set up a "city" under the sea. A five-room "house" was built in a garage workshop and lowered into the water off Port
5 Sudan in the Red Sea. For twenty-nine days, five men lived at a depth of forty feet. At a much lower level, two more divers stayed for a week in a smaller "house." On returning to the surface, the men said that they had experienced no difficulty in breathing
10 and had made many interesting scientific observations. The leader of the party, Commander Cousteau, spoke of the possibility of cultivating the seabed. He said that if permanent stations were set up under the sea, underwater farms could provide food for the
15 growing population of the world.

The divers in both "houses" spent most of their time exploring the depths of the sea. On four occasions they went down to 360 feet and observed many extraordinary forms of sea life, some of which
20 had never been seen before. It was possible to move rapidly underwater in a special vessel known as a "diving saucer." During their stay, Commander Cousteau and diver Andre Falco reached a depth of 1,000 feet and witnessed a gathering of an immense
25 colony of crabs which numbered perhaps hundreds of millions.

### Instructions

In not more than 80 words, describe how the divers spent their time under the sea.

**Main Points** | **Connectors**

1. Five divers—29 days—house. ⎤
2. 40 feet under sea. ⎦ *at a depth*

3. Another two—week—house—
   deeper level.                    ] *Meanwhile*
4. Explored depths.                 ]
5. 360 feet—four times.             | *and*
6. Saw strange forms, sea life.     ] *where*
7. Cousteau and Falco—saucer—       ] *During their stay*
   1,000 feet.
8. Millions of crabs.               ] *where*

# Section 4

## .... COMPREHENSION AND ....
## COMPOSITION

## To the teacher

### 1. Aims

(a) To enable the students to apply all that they have learned about sentence structure and word order.

(b) To enable the students to join sentences with conjunctions, participles and other connecting words, without teacher assistance.

(c) To test the students' understanding of the text *(Comprehension)*.

(d) To provide the students with practice in explaining words and phrases as they are used in the text *(Vocabulary)*.

(e) To enable the students to distinguish between essential and nonessential material so that they will be able to write a carefully ordered summary on their own.

(f) To provide practice in writing simple essays which, in this section, take the form of continuation or reproduction exercises.

### 2. How the student should work

This section has been divided into two parts, each consisting of ten passages. Each passage is just over

350 words in length and consists of three paragraphs. For the most part, comprehension and vocabulary questions are confined to the first two paragraphs and summary-writing assignments to the last paragraph. The method for writing summaries differs slightly in each of the two parts of the section.

(a) **Comprehension** The student should be trained to give a short answer to each question in one complete sentence. This means that part of the question must be incorporated in each answer. If, for instance, the question is "Why did the man return to the hotel?" the answer should not be "Because he had forgotten his coat," but "The man returned to the hotel because he had forgotten his coat." In answering questions, students sometimes have a tendency to ignore tenses. They should therefore be taught to pay attention to the structure of questions and to use the same tense construction in answers.

(b) **Vocabulary** Dictionary definitions should *not* be given. Words should be explained as they are used in the text by means of synonyms or equivalent phrases. The student should be trained to replace the word in the text with the word or phrase chosen, to see if it fits into the context. Only one "explanation" (word or phrase) should be given for each word or phrase listed in the vocabulary exercise.

(c) **Summaries** In the first ten passages of this section, there is a return to the question-answer technique, but with one important difference—the student should give note-form answers to the questions in order to formulate the "main points." Then the student should join these main points together to write the summary, referring to the passage as necessary. The purpose of the brackets to the right of the questions is to help the student see ways of joining sentences. They may, however, be ignored, and the student's own ideas for joining answers may be followed. Conjunctions and other connecting words are not supplied in the exercises in this section and, therefore, must be added by the student. At the end of each summary, the student should mark down the number of words used in writing the summary. Articles, pronouns and compound words count as single words. A summary may be written in fewer than the required number of words (80 words), but this word limit should not be exceeded.

(d) **Essays** Students should be encouraged to write the assigned compositions within their vocabulary range without the aid of a dictionary. Since the titles of essays are closely based on the passages, students should use as many as they can of the words and phrases contained in the text of the reading. Essays should be limited to two or three paragraphs. At this stage, more emphasis should be placed on correct English than on subject matter and the orderly presentation of ideas.

### 3. Vocabulary range

The student's passive vocabulary should be in the region of 2,000 words. A further 400 words have been added to the actual range, bringing the total up to 1,800 words.

### 4. Structures

A reasonable working knowledge of all the more common structures has been assumed. Highly involved sentences and unfamiliar constructions have been avoided.

## To the student

In this section you will be applying all you have learned about simple, compound and complex sentences. The study material provided in this section of the book includes the following: reading passages, comprehension questions, vocabulary review, summary writing and essay assignments.

### How to work

1. **Reading Passages** Read each passage carefully two or three times.

2. **Comprehension Questions** Following each reading passage, you will be asked to answer a number of questions to demonstrate that you have understood the passage. In answering these questions, keep the following points in mind:

   (a) First, read the question carefully.

   (b) Then, look at the reading passage again and locate the particular phrase or sentence that answers the question.

   (c) Finally, using the information from the passage, write an answer to the question in your own words.

   (d) Remember that each of the answers you write should be one complete sentence.

   (e) Remember, also, that your answer should use the same verb tense that was used in the question.

   (f) Number each of your answers (1, 2, . . .).

3. **Vocabulary Reviews** In these exercises, you will be asked to show that you understand certain words and phrases in the reading passage by supplying other words or phrases with similar meanings. A line reference number is given with each word or phrase in the Vocabulary Review so that you can refer to the passage to see how the word or phrase is used.

4. **Summaries** You will be asked to write a carefully ordered summary of a portion of each reading passage. In connection with the exercises in summary writing in Section 3 of this book, you were given a list of "Main Points" and were asked to join them together to form a paragraph. In this section, Section 4, you will be expected to find the "main points" yourself. Follow these procedures:

   (a) Read the instructions to find out exactly what portion of the reading passage your summary should cover; that is, find out where your summary should begin and end.

   (b) Reread the portion of the reading passage that you will be using for your summary.

(c)    Look at the list of questions given in the book and answer each question in note form in order to develop your "main points."

(d)    Notice that there are large brackets on the right side of the list of questions given in the book. These brackets show you which of your "main points" may be joined together to form a single sentence; you will of course need to supply appropriate connection words to join the "main points." If you prefer, you may ignore the brackets and join the "main points" in your own way.

(e)    In joining the "main points" to form sentences, you may refer to the reading passage as often as necessary, but you should try to use your own words in your answer. All of your sentences together should form a one-paragraph summary.

(f)    Read through your completed summary and correct any mistakes you may have made.

(g)    At the end of the summary, mark down the exact number of words you have used. The word limit for each summary is 80 words. You may write fewer than 80 words, but you should not go above this limit.

(h)    Give your summary a title.

5.   **Essays** The assignments for essays are based on material contained in the reading passages. In writing the essays, you should not refer to a dictionary. Try to use as many of the words and phrases found in the reading passages as you can.

The following is a sample lesson which illustrates the procedures you should use in this section with reading passages 61 to 70. Before you begin your first assignment, work through this sample lesson carefully to be sure you understand all of the procedures.

### Example

Hidden passengers traveling in ships, on trains, or even in cars can be a terrible nuisance—especially

difference between human beings and insects. The
5 former make every possible effort to avoid discovery,
while the latter quickly draw attention to themselves.

   We can only sympathize with the unfortunate man
in Washington who had to stop his car soon after
starting out from Yakima to drive to Ellensburg. Hear-
10 ing a strange noise from the back of the car, he naturally got out to take a look. He examined the wheels
carefully, but since he found nothing wrong, he continued on his way. The noise began almost immediately and now it was louder than ever. Quickly turning
15 his head to look back, the man saw what appeared to
be a great black cloud following the car. When he
stopped at a gas station farther on, he was told that a
queen bee must be hidden somewhere in his car since
there were thousands of bees nearby.
20    On learning this, the man realized that the only way
to escape would be to drive away quickly and then to
drive as fast as possible. After an hour's hard driving,
he arrived in Ellensburg where he parked his car outside a small cafe and went in to have coffee. It was not
25 long before someone who had seen him arrive hurried
in to inform him that his car was covered with bees.
The poor driver telephoned the police and explained
what had happened. The police decided that the best
way to deal with the situation would be to call a local
30 beekeeper. In a short time, the beekeeper arrived. He
found the unwelcome passenger hidden near the rear
axle of the car. Very grateful to the driver for this unexpected gift, the beekeeper took the queen and her
thousands of followers home in a large box. Equally
35 grateful, the driver drove away in peace, at last free
from the "black cloud" which had hung over his car.


## 1. Comprehension

   In your own words, give short answers to these
questions. Use one complete sentence for each
answer.

   (a)  How do human beings differ from insects when
        they hide in ships, trains or cars?

Why did the man stop his car soon after he had started out from Yakima to drive to Ellensburg?

(c) What did the man see when he turned to look back?

## 2. Vocabulary

Give another word or phrase to replace the following words as they are used in the passage: terrible (2); especially (2); avoid (5); discovery (5); sympathize (7); unfortunate (7); immediately (13).

## 3. Summary

In not more than 80 words, describe what happened after the driver found out that a queen bee must have been hidden in his car. Use your own words. Do not include anything that is not in the last paragraph of the reading passage (Lines 20-36).

Answer these questions in note form to get your "main points."

1. What did the man do to escape the bees?
2. What town did he arrive in?
3. What did he do there?
4. What did someone tell him?
5. Who did the driver call?
6. Who did they send?
7. Where did he find the queen bee?
8. What did the beekeeper do with the queen and her followers?
9. What did the driver do then?

## 4. Essay

Write a composition in about 200 words on *one* of the following:
(a) Imagine that the beekeeper did not arrive. Describe what the driver did.
(b) Write a story about a person who hides in a lifeboat on board a big ship.

**Possible answers**

## 1. Comprehension

(a) When they hide in ships, on trains or in cars, human beings do all they can to avoid being found, while insects attract attention.

(b) The man stopped his car soon after he had started out from Yakima to drive to Ellensburg because he heard a peculiar noise.

(c) When he turned to look back, the man saw something that looked like a big dark cloud.

## 2. Vocabulary

terrible: awful
especially: particularly
avoid: escape
discovery: being found
sympathize: feel sorry for
unfortunate: unlucky
immediately: at once

## 3. Summary

| **Main Points** | **Connectors** |
|---|---|
| 1. Drove away quickly. | *In order to* |
| 2. Arrived Ellensburg. | *and after some time* |
| 3. Parked car—cafe— coffee. | *Parking* |
| 4. Someone told him: bees—car. | *When* |
| 5. Called police. | |
| 6. Sent beekeeper. | |
| 7. Found queen bee near axle. | *who* |
| 8. Took queen and bees home—box. | |
| 9. Driver drove away. | *and* |

## The Hidden Passenger

*In order to* escape the bees, the driver drove away quickly *and after some time* arrived in Ellensburg. *Parking* his car outside a cafe, he went in to have coffee. *When* someone told him that his car was covered with bees, the driver telephoned the police. They sent a beekeeper *who* soon found the queen bee near the rear axle. He took the queen and her followers home in a box, *and* the driver then drove away in peace.

(80 Words)

### 4. Essay

The essay-writing assignment suggests two different topics for an essay. Since you will be writing an essay in your own words, no example can be provided in this sample lesson.

This year I decided to do something to regain my reputation as a good uncle. My nephew, Tony, had never forgiven me for the dictionary I had bought him as a birthday present last year. His parents had no
5 reason to be grateful to me either, because the year before, I had presented their dear son with a jar of paste, some funny pictures and a scrapbook. Instead of pasting the pictures in the scrapbook, Tony had naturally covered every wall in the house with them.
10 This year, therefore, I decided to let him choose for himself.

We went into a big toy store but Tony found something wrong with everything he saw. I showed him toy after toy, but to no avail; he saw nothing he liked.
15 Then suddenly I saw his eyes light up. He had discovered something he really did want: a large tin drum. I was quite pleased too—until I thought about what Tony's mother would say when she saw it. Nobody would get any sleep for weeks! I led Tony
20 away quickly, saying that the drum was too expensive. If that was how I felt, Tony replied jokingly, then I could buy him the big model train set in the store

window. Now that was *really* expensive, so I quickly changed the subject.

25 Tony asked if he could look around by himself for a while, and I made the most of my opportunity to sit down and rest my aching feet. Fifteen minutes passed but there was still no sign of Tony. I wondered where he was and got up to look for him. I asked a young

30 lady if she had seen a little boy in jeans and a T-shirt. She looked about her helplessly and pointed out that there were so many little boys in jeans. I was beginning to get worried when I saw an odd figure dressed in strange purple clothes. It was Tony, of course. He

35 was wearing a false beard and had a caveman's axe in one hand, and a space gun in the other. He informed me that he was the first caveman to fly in space.

### 1.  Comprehension

In your own words, give short answers to these questions. Use one complete sentence for each answer.

(a)  Why had Tony never forgiven his uncle?

(b)  What had Tony done with the funny pictures his uncle had given him?

(c)  Why did Tony's uncle decide not to buy the tin drum?

### 2.  Vocabulary

Give another word or phrase to replace the following words and phrases as they are used in the passage: regain (1); reputation (2); parents (4); to be grateful to (5); funny (7); too expensive (20).

### 3.  Summary

In not more than 80 words, give an account of the writer's experiences from the moment Tony began looking around by himself. Use your own words. Do not include anything that is not in the last paragraph of the reading (Lines 25-38).

Answer these questions in note form to get your main points:

1. Why did the writer sit down after Tony went off? ]
2. Did Tony return very soon or not? ]
3. Did the writer look for him or not? ]
4. What did the writer do when he could not find him? ]
5. Could the lady help him find Tony? ]
6. Did the writer see an odd figure or not? ]
7. Who was it? ]
8. How was he dressed? ]
9. What did he have in each hand? ]
10. How did Tony describe himself? ]

### 4. Essay

Write a composition in about 200 words on *one* of the following:

(a) Pretend that the writer had not been able to find his nephew so easily. Describe what he did.

(b) Imagine that the writer bought the tin drum that Tony wanted. Describe what happened after they returned home.

 Percy's mysterious disappearance upset everybody a great deal. Percy is a performer in a nightclub and just before he was due to appear on stage, it was discovered that he was not in his usual place. There
5 was certainly good cause for worry because Percy is a dangerous snake about six feet long.

The search for Percy lasted several days, and a great many people joined in. Since Percy could not possibly have gone out into the street, everybody
10 realized that he was hiding somewhere in the club. The searchers found that some of the boards in Percy's room had rotted and there was a gap in the floor. It seemed likely that Percy had slipped under

the floor and then crawled behind a wall where the
15 central heating unit was located.

The manager of the club suggested that Percy
might have found some mice to eat under the floor. If
so, he would have probably curled up around the
warm pipes and gone to sleep. Since a snake that has
20 had a satisfying meal can sleep for several days
continuously, a determined effort had to be made to
get him out. The central heating unit was therefore
turned off immediately and the temperature in the
room fell to a few degrees above zero. But Percy, who
25 has the reputation of being a lazy creature, made no
attempt to come out. The manager then tried
something else. He placed a dish full of tasty
delicacies near the broken floorboards. But still Percy
failed to appear. With the hot water turned off, it was
30 decided that Percy must be freezing by now, so an
electric heater was put into his room to encourage
him to come in and warm himself. To help him make
up his mind even more quickly, cold air was blown
under the floorboards. Even these measures did not
35 succeed, so there was only one thing left to do. The
next morning, the whole wall was carefully taken
down brick by brick so as not to frighten Percy with
too much noise. The hot water pipes were gradually
uncovered, but to their astonishment, the searchers
40 found no sign of Percy anywhere.

## 1. Comprehension

In your own words, give short answers to these
questions. Use one complete sentence for each
answer.

(a) Why was everybody worried when Percy
disappeared?

(b) How long did the search for Percy last?

(c) Why did the searchers believe that Percy had
hidden behind the wall?

## 2. Vocabulary

Give another word or phrase to replace the following words and phrases as they are used in the pas-

sage: a great deal (2); discovered (4); certainly (5); cause (5); joined in (8); rotted (12); gap (12).

### 3. Summary

In not more than 80 words, describe what the searchers did to find Percy. Use your own words. Do not include anything that is not in the last paragraph of the reading (Lines 16-40).

Answer these questions in note form to get your main points:
1. Was the room warm or cold after the heating unit was turned off?
2. Did Percy appear or not?
3. What was placed near the broken floorboards?
4. What was put into the room when Percy still had not appeared?
5. Where was cold air directed?
6. Did these measures succeed or not?
7. What did the searchers do the next morning?
8. Why were they surprised when they uncovered the hot water pipes?

### 4. Essay

Write a composition in about 200 words on *one* of the following:
  (a) Describe how the search for Percy continued and how he was finally found.
  (b) Imagine that Percy had really been hiding someplace in the nightclub after all. Describe the scene that evening when he suddenly appeared and frightened the customers.

**63**

The four famous rock stars were due to arrive at any moment and a large crowd of young people had gathered at the airport to welcome them. The police found it very difficult to keep the crowd under control
5 after the plane landed and the performers appeared. They smiled and waved cheerfully at everybody. Dressed in pink shirts and light blue trousers, and with their long hair and their musical instruments over their shoulders, the four young men looked
10 remarkably alike.

In spite of the large number of policemen present, it was clear that the group would not be able to get to their waiting car easily. Word had gotten out that they had composed a new song which would be heard
15 when they performed at the auditorium that evening. They were now greeted with cries of "Play something! Play your new song!"

Even the police looked pleased when the young men unstrapped their instruments and prepared to do
20 one of their numbers as the price for getting out of the airport. The crowd settled down and listened to the first performance of the new song. As soon as it was over, there was a great burst of applause and then everyone started stamping and shouting. Several
25 young women fainted and had to be carried away by the rescue unit which was standing by. Greedy for

more, the crowd demanded a repeat performance. Once again the performers yielded, but when the crowd requested still another song, the group
30 cheerfully but firmly refused. Now, closely surrounded by the police, they put away their instruments and started towards their car which was some distance away. The crowd pushed forward, but policemen, locked arm in arm, prevented anyone from
35 getting through. It took the singers a long time to reach their car. Finally, however, they got in and were just about to drive away when a young woman, who had somehow managed to get past the police, jumped onto the roof of the car. She shouted loudly as two
40 policemen dragged her away and the car began moving slowly through the cheering crowd.

## 1. Comprehension

In your own words, give short answers to these questions. Use one complete sentence for each answer.

    (a)   Why had a large crowd gathered at the airport?

    (b)   Why did the young men look so much alike?

    (c)   What did everyone expect to hear that evening when the rock group performed at the auditorium?

## 2. Vocabulary

Give another word or phrase to replace the following words and phrases as they are used in the passage: famous (1); due to (1); gathered (3); under control (4); looked alike (9-10); word had gotten out (13).

## 3. Summary

In not more than 80 words, describe what happened at the airport from the moment the young men were asked to give a repeat performance until they drove away. Use your own words. Do not include anything that is not in the last paragraph of the reading (Lines 18-41).

Answer these questions in note form to get your main points:

1. Were the musicians asked to give a repeat performance or not?
2. Did they agree to do it?
3. Did they agree to play for a third time, or did they refuse?
4. What did they do with their musical instruments?
5. Where did they go?
6. How did the police prevent the crowd from getting through to the musicians?
7. What did a young woman do when they were just going to drive away?
8. What did two policemen do then?
9. Did the car start moving or not?

## 4. Essay

Write a composition in about 200 words on *one* of the following:

(a) Imagine that the crowd managed to push past the police. Describe the scene that took place.
(b) Describe the performance given by the musicians later that evening at the auditorium.

There was great public interest when a sunken area mysteriously appeared in the middle of a field. Army engineers and specialists were called in to explain how it had gotten there. They offered various explana-
5 tions but were not at all sure how the bowl-shaped depression had been caused. It was thought that a large shell which must have been buried in the ground for many years had suddenly exploded, but it was not possible to prove this.
10 A "simple," but highly improbable, explanation was offered by a man who claims to know a great deal about UFOs—the strange "unidentified flying objects" which are round in shape and are said to visit earth occasionally from outer space. This man's

94

15 explanation may have been nonsense, but at least it was imaginative. At any rate, it was far more interesting than the one given by the army people.

After examining the ground carefully, the man claimed to have seen special marks on the soil quite
20 near the sunken area. These, he said, could only have been caused by a spaceship. Moreover, the leaves on some bushes nearby had turned yellow because of a strange gas which had come from the outer space vehicle just before it landed. Even a tree some
25 distance away appeared to have been burned slightly. A small piece of metal found in the cavity itself provided further proof that a strange object had been there. According to the UFO "specialist," it was quite clear that people from another world had been
30 circling the earth trying to pick up information and apparently on one of their orbits something went wrong. Because of this they had been forced to land in the field so that the malfunction could be corrected. The sunken area had been caused when
35 the spaceship struck the earth, while the strange marks nearby were made when it lifted off again. This, said the man, was the simplest explanation of how the crater had appeared. Judging from the interest the public took in the matter, there must have been quite
40 a few people who secretly believed or hoped that this "simple" explanation was the true one.

### 1. Comprehension

In your own words, give short answers to these questions. Use one complete sentence for each answer.

(a) Why were army engineers and specialists called in?

(b) How did they think the sunken area had been caused?

(c) What are UFOs?

### 2. Vocabulary

Give another word or phrase to replace the following words and phrases as they are used in the passage: offered (4); various (4); exploded (8); highly (10); improbable (10); at any rate (16).

### 3. Summary

How did the man "prove" that a spaceship had visited earth?

Using your own words, write a summary in not more than 80 words. Do not include anything that is not in the last paragraph of the reading (Lines 18-41).

Answer these questions in note form to get your main points:

1. What did the man see near the sunken area? ⌐
2. Why had the leaves on some bushes nearby turned yellow? ⌐
3. What had happened to a tree? ⌐
4. What did the man find in the cavity? ⌐
5. What had happened when the spaceship was circling the earth? ⌐
6. Why did it have to land? ⌐
7. How had the crater been made? ⌐
8. How had the strange marks been caused? ⌐

### 4. Essay

Write a composition in about 200 words on *one* of the following:

(a) Pretend that the man's explanation was the true one. Describe what happened when the spaceship landed in the field.

(b) Write an essay explaining how the sunken area (crater) was caused. Your explanation should be different from those given in the reading passage.

Whenever I go to Santa Monica, I stay at the Grand Hotel. In spite of its name, it is not very grand, but it is cheap, clean and comfortable. What is more, I know the manager well, so I never have to go to the trouble
5 of making a reservation. The fact that I always get the same room never fails to surprise me. It is located at

the far end of the building and overlooks the beautiful marina.

On my last visit, the manager told me that I could
10 have my usual room, but he added apologetically that I might find it a little noisy. The demand for rooms was so great, he told me, that the management had decided to build a new wing. I did not mind this at all. It amused me to think that the dear old Grand Hotel
15 was making a determined effort to live up to its name.

During the first day, I hardly noticed the noise at all. The room was a little dusty, but that was to be expected. The following afternoon, I bought a paperback at the newsstand in the lobby and went
20 upstairs to read. I had no sooner sat down than I heard someone hammering loudly on the wall. At first I paid no attention to it, but after a while I began to feel very uncomfortable. My clothes were slowly being covered with fine white powder. Soon there was so
25 much dust in the room that I began to cough. The hammering was now louder than ever, and bits of plaster were coming off the walls. It seemed as though the whole building was going to fall! I went downstairs immediately to complain to the manager.
30 We both returned to my room but everything was very quiet. As we stood there looking at each other, I felt rather ashamed of myself for having dragged him all the way up to the room for nothing. All of a sudden, the hammering began again and a large brick landed
35 on the floor. Looking up near the ceiling, we saw that a sledgehammer had forced its way through the wall, making a very large hole right above my bed!

## 1. Comprehension

In your own words, give short answers to these questions. Use one complete sentence for each answer.

(a) Why does the writer never have to go to the trouble of making a reservation at the Grand Hotel?

(b) Where was the writer's room located?

(c) Why did the manager think that the writer would find the room a little noisy?

## 2. Vocabulary

Give another word or phrase to replace the following words and phrases as they are used in the passage: grand (2); cheap (3); surprise (6); located (6); it amused me (14); effort (15); name (15).

## 3. Summary

In not more than 80 words, describe what happened in the hotel room from the moment the writer went upstairs to read. Use your own words. Do not include anything that is not in the last paragraph of the reading (Lines 16-37).

Answer these questions in note form to get your main points:

1. Where did the writer go after he had bought a book?
2. What did he hear after sitting down?
3. What were his clothes covered with?
4. Did he begin to cough or not?
5. What was coming off the walls?
6. Why did the writer go downstairs?
7. Was there any noise when they returned?
8. What fell on the floor when the hammering began?
9. What made a hole in the wall?

## 4. Essay

Write a composition in about 200 words on *one* of the following:

(a) Imagine you are the person in the story. Write a continuation of the story.
(b) Describe a visit to the hotel the following year just after the new wing has been completed.

Checks have largely replaced money as a means of exchange since they are widely accepted everywhere. Although this is very convenient for both buyer and seller, it should not be forgotten that checks are not
5 real money; they are quite valueless in themselves. Store managers always run a certain risk when they accept a check and they certainly cannot be blamed if, on occasion, they refuse to accept one.

People do not always understand this and are quite
10 shocked if their good faith is questioned. For example, an old and very wealthy friend of mine told me he had an extremely unpleasant experience recently. He went to a famous jewelry store that carries a large stock of precious stones and asked to
15 be shown some pearl necklaces. After examining several trays, he decided to buy a particularly valuable string of pearls and asked if he could pay by check. The clerk said that this was quite acceptable, but the moment my friend signed his name, he was ushered
20 into the manager's office.

The manager was very polite, but he explained that someone with exactly the same name had presented them with a worthless check not long ago. My friend got very angry when he heard this and said he would
25 buy a necklace somewhere else. When he got up to go, the manager told him that the police would arrive at any moment and that he had better stay unless he wanted to get into serious trouble. Sure enough, the police arrived almost immediately. They apologized to
30 my friend for the inconvenience, but explained that someone using that name was responsible for passing quite a number of bad checks to downtown stores. Then they asked him for two pieces of identification, such as a driver's license and a credit card, but
35 unfortunately he had nothing with him except his checkbook. Fortunately for my friend, his bank was just three blocks away, and the bank manager was only too happy to respond to my friend's telephone request to come to the store right away to identify
40 him.

### 1. Comprehension

In your own words, give short answers to these questions. Use one complete sentence for each answer.

(a) Why do store managers always run a certain risk when they accept a check?

(b) What did the man decide to buy?

(c) When was the man ushered into the manager's office?

### 2. Vocabulary

Give another word or phrase to replace the following words and phrases as they are used in the passage: largely (1); convenient (3); valueless (5); on occasion (8); wealthy (11); extremely (12); acceptable (18).

### 3. Summary

In not more than 80 words, describe the man's experiences in the jewelry store after he was ushered into the manager's office. Use your own words. Do not include anything that is not in the last paragraph of the reading (Lines 21-40).

Answer these questions in note form to get your main points:

1. What did the man learn from the manager?
2. Did he get angry or not?
3. Why was he not supposed to leave the store?
4. What did the police explain to the man?
5. Did they ask him for some form of identification or not?
6. How far was my friend's bank from the store?
7. Was the bank manager willing to come to the store to identify him or not?

### 4. Essay

Write a composition in about 200 words on *one* of the following:

(a) Describe how the man who had been passing

bad checks was caught in the same store.

(b) Pretend that the man who wanted to buy the necklace was really the one who had been passing bad checks. Describe how he was caught by the police.

**67** Homer, the great blind poet of ancient Greece, wrote a long account of the Trojan war in the *Iliad*. People had long been interested in finding the city of Troy, but the only man who took Homer's description
5 seriously was Heinrich Schliemann. Using Homer as his guide, Schliemann discovered what was almost certainly the ancient city of Troy. Though he had made it his aim to find Troy as a young man, Schliemann was only able to realize his ambition after he
10 had amassed a large fortune and retired from business.

Schliemann at once realized that the spot in Asia Minor generally believed to be Troy did not match Homer's detailed description. According to Homer, a
15 palace of sixty rooms had been built on a hill, and the Greeks had marched between their ships and the city several times a day. The hill on which Troy was supposed to have been built was not only very small, but was a great distance from the sea as well.

20 Much nearer the sea, Schliemann came across a bigger hill. Homer had written that Achilles and Hector had run around the walls of Troy three times while fighting each other. Having calculated that this would have been possible, Schliemann decided to
25 dig. It was not long before he discovered the remains of a city—not Troy, but a much later one called New Ilium. When his workmen dug deeper, Schliemann was most surprised to find that there were no less than nine cities built on top of each other. But which
30 of these was Troy? Homer again provided Schliemann with two important facts: the city had been built of stone and had been burned to the ground by the conquering Greeks. Schliemann believed that the second city must have been Troy, for he found the

35 ruins of a palace and a large gate blackened by fire.
Yet the most astonishing discovery was still to come.
After noticing something shining in the soil,
Schliemann got so excited that he dug with his bare
hands. He unearthed the beautifully preserved treas-
40 ure of King Priam: gold, silver and jewelry, thus com-
pleting one of the most important historical discover-
ies ever made.

### 1. Comprehension

In your own words, give short answers to these
questions. Use one complete sentence for each
answer.

(a) What use did Schliemann make of Homer's
*Iliad*?
(b) When was Schliemann able to realize his
ambitions?
(c) Why would it not have been possible for the
Greeks to march to the sea several times a day
from the small hill on which Troy was supposed to have been built?

### 2. Vocabulary

Give another word or phrase to replace the following words and phrases as they are used in the passage: account (2); ancient (7); aim (8); realized (12);
did not match (13); supposed (18).

### 3. Summary

In not more than 80 words, describe how Schliemann discovered the city of Troy. Use your own
words. Do not include anything that is not in the last
paragraph of the reading (Lines 20-42).

Answer these questions in note form to get your
main points:

1. What did Schliemann see near the sea?
2. Did he calculate that it would have been possible
to run around it or not?
3. What was the name of the city he found after
digging?

4. How many cities did he find in all?
5. What did the discovery of a palace and a large gate blackened by fire tell him?
6. What did he notice in the soil?
7. Did he dig with a shovel or with his bare hands?
8. What did he find?

## 4. Essay

Write a composition in about 200 words on *one* of the following:

(a) Imagine that Schliemann is telling his own story. Write a first-person account.

(b) Describe any important discovery of the same type that has been made in some country that you know about.

The first man to jump out of an airplane traveling at a speed greater than sound was Arthur Ray Hawkins, an outstanding U.S. Navy pilot. Jumps of this sort had long been regarded as impossible.

5 During an air show over Mississippi in 1954, Hawkins was flying an entirely new type of plane. At 40,000 feet, the nose of the plane dipped sharply. No matter how hard he tried, Hawkins could not pull it out of the dive, and it gathered such speed that it was soon
10 traveling faster than the speed of sound. Strapped in his seat, and hanging almost upside down, the pilot could not reach the control which would open the canopy. Near him, however, there was another control which was to be used only in case of emergency.
15 Hawkins pulled it. There was a sudden explosion and still in his seat—which shielded him to some extent— he was ejected through the glass canopy above his head.

While still half-conscious, Hawkins tried to pull the
20 cord which would open his parachute. It was fortunate that he failed in his attempt, for at such a rate of speed, the parachute would have been torn to pieces. As he was diving towards earth, he realized that the

supply hose which was connected to the oxygen
25 system had of course been torn away. Rapidly losing
consciousness because of lack of oxygen, he knew
that he had to open the parachute—otherwise, he
might not get another chance to do it. At about 29,000
feet, the parachute opened and Hawkins pulled a
30 handle which freed him from the pilot seat. Swinging
through the air, he was trembling with cold and he
began to black out. There was not enough oxygen at
that altitude! Just then, he remembered the technique
for breathing at high altitude. He took short, sharp
35 breaths, thus forcing air into the bloodstream. This
kept him alive until, at 10,000 feet, he could begin to
breathe without difficulty. Soon afterwards, he landed
safely in a cotton field. His plane crashed in some
woods nearby, but luckily no one was hurt.

## 1. Comprehension

In your own words, give short answers to these
questions.
  (a) Where did the air show take place?
  (b) Why did the airplane travel faster than the
      speed of sound?
  (c) Why was Hawkins unable to reach the control
      which would open the canopy?

## 2. Vocabulary

Give another word or phrase to replace the following words and phrases as they are used in the passage: at a speed greater than (2); outstanding (3); regarded (4); entirely (6); type (6); shielded (16); to some
extent (16).

## 3. Summary

In not more than 80 words, describe Hawkins's
experiences after he was ejected from the airplane.
Use your own words. Do not include anything that is
not in the last paragraph of the reading (Lines 19-39).
Answer these questions in note form to get your
main points:

1. Why was it lucky that Hawkins failed to open his parachute after he left the plane?
2. Why did he open the parachute at 29,000 feet?
3. Did he begin to lose consciousness after he freed himself from the pilot seat or not?
4. How did he breathe at this altitude?
5. When was he able to breathe easily?
6. Where did he land?

## 4. Essay

Write a composition in about 200 words on *one* of the following:

   (a) Pretend that you had to parachute from an airplane. Describe your experiences.
   (b) Your first landing on the moon.

Some people seem to have been born with an unfailing sense of direction. Even when lost in the woods, they find their way home as surely as an animal picks up the scent of its prey. The secret is
5 probably that they never *feel* lost. Others, myself included, can manage to get lost even in a department store.

When I was in the army, there was nothing I disliked more than the course in map reading, for the simple
10 reason that I *always* feel lost—even with a map in my hand. For weeks I had been lying awake at night

thinking of the practical test I would have to face at the end of the course. Finally, the dreaded day arrived. It was to be my responsibility to lead a small
15 squad of soldiers back to camp from the middle of nowhere. We were driven out in a closed truck and left in a cow pasture with instructions to get back to camp as quickly as possible.

Knowing about my problem as they did, the soldiers
20 smiled as they saw me looking at the map and they made all sorts of "helpful" suggestions. I folded the map up, put it in my pocket, and announced that we would head east. After walking through cornfields for over an hour, we came to a wide stream. I again
25 looked at the map. It seemed to be covered with masses of thin blue lines, but which particular line was *this* stream? In frustration, we sat down to rest in the shade and I felt like throwing the map into the water. About fifteen minutes later, a boat came along
30 and I asked the owner of the boat if he could give us a lift to the nearest town. I pretended that we had been out for a hike and somehow gotten lost. The owner of the boat invited us aboard and I felt very foolish when he told me that he had helped hundreds of soldiers
35 pass their map-reading test! Not long afterwards, we got off the boat and, following the boat owner's instructions, took a bus into town. When we got back to camp, my company commander congratulated me on having led the men back so quickly!

### 1. Comprehension

In your own words, give short answers to these questions. Use one complete sentence for each answer.

    (a) Why, in the writer's opinion, do some people have a good sense of direction?

    (b) What would the writer be required to do at the end of the course in map reading?

    (c) How did the writer and the soldiers reach the cow pasture?

## 2. Vocabulary

Give another word or phrase to replace the following words as they are used in the reading passage: unfailing (2); woods (3); scent (4); disliked (8); test (12); dreaded (13); responsibility (14).

## Summary

In not more than 80 words, describe how the soldiers got back to camp from the moment the writer put the map in his pocket. Use your own words. Do not include anything that is not in the last paragraph of the reading (Lines 19-39).

Answer these questions in note form to get your main points:

1. Did the writer put the map away or not?
2. In which direction did he lead the squad?
3. Did they march through cornfields or not?
4. What did they find?
5. Could the writer find the stream on the map?
6. Did they sit down in the shade or not?
7. What happened after a few minutes?
8. What did the writer ask the owner of the boat?
9. Were they invited on board or not?
10. What did the owner of the boat tell them to do when they got off?
11. Did they get back to camp very quickly or not?

## 4. Essay

Write a composition in about 200 words on *one* of the following:

(a) Describe how the writer was given a second test and how this time he failed completely to find his way back to camp.

(b) Imagine that the company commander found out that the owner of the boat had been helping soldiers in their map-reading test. Describe what he did.

Hunting was originally a means of providing food, but it has now become a sport. Although in some parts of the world there are still people who hunt wild animals to provide themselves with food, in many
5 countries hunting is as much a social activity as anything else.

A great many years ago, fishermen in Japan used birds to catch fish. This art of fishing is said to be at least a thousand years old and is mentioned in
10 Japanese Noh plays. Today, however, fishing in this way has simply become a sport, since those who fish in this way are not seriously interested in catching fish.

On summer nights, the fishing boats set out on
15 rivers in various locations. At the front of each boat there is an iron basket in which a wood fire is kept burning. As the graceful curved boats float past, carried along by the current, these fires, dotted here and there, make bright patterns on the water. Steering
20 down the river, the fishermen beat the sides of the boat to encourage the birds, and people out for an evening's entertainment either sit or lie on the floor of the boats drinking *saki* and sometimes cooking a meal for themselves over the flames of the fire. This
25 method of fishing demands great skill because the fisherman has to handle three or four birds in one hand. A long piece of string is tied around the neck of each bird and the fisherman must take great care to keep the birds separated from each other. Every so
30 often, the birds are turned loose and they fly close to the water in search of fish. The moment a bird catches a fish in its beak, it is pulled back into the boat. The string is held tightly around the bird's throat to prevent it from swallowing the fish it has caught.
35 When there do not seem to be many fish in the river, the fishermen can sometimes be seen secretly throwing dead fish into the water for the birds to catch. No one really objects to this practice since it is all part of this unusual sport.

## 1. Comprehension

In your own words, give short answers to these questions. Use one complete sentence for each answer.

(a) What was the original purpose of hunting?

(b) Why are the Japanese fishermen mentioned in this reading passage not seriously interested in catching fish?

(c) What time of the year do these fishing boats go out?

## 2. Vocabulary

Give another word or phrase to replace the following words as they are used in the reading passage: originally (1); means (1); provide (4); mentioned (9); various (15); beat (20); skill (25).

## 3. Summary

In not more than 80 words, give an account of this art of fishing from line 19 (Steering down the river, . . .) to the end of the passage. Use your own words. Do not include anything that is not in the last paragraph of the reading (Lines 14–39).

Answer these questions in note form to get your main points:

1. What do the fishermen do to encourage the birds? ⎤
   ⎦

2. How many birds does the fisherman have in one hand? ⎤
   ⎥
   ⎥
3. What is tied around the neck of each bird? ⎥
   ⎥
4. What must the fisherman take great care to do? ⎦

5. What does the fisherman do after the bird catches a fish? ⎤
   ⎥
6. Why is the string held tightly? ⎦

7. What do the fishermen sometimes throw into the water? ⎤
   ⎥
8. Why do they have to do this? ⎦

### 4. Essay

Write a composition in about 200 words on *one* of the following:

(a)  Imagine a fisherman describing this sport to you. Write an account of what he has told you.

(b)  The first time you went fishing.


## To the teacher

In this second part of Section 4, comprehension, vocabulary review and summary assignments are of the same type as those given with passages 61-70. At this stage, however, the student will be expected to write a summary entirely on his or her own. The student should be asked to follow the instructions given below. The student's work in summary writing will include three distinct steps: (a) making a list of "points," (b) writing a rough draft and (c) preparing a final copy.


## To the student

Comprehension questions, vocabulary and essay assignments will be no different from those encountered in the first part of this section. Now, however, you will be asked to write summaries entirely on your own—including the formulation of a series of questions, the development of "main points," and the writing of a summary. In carrying out the assignments for passages 71 to 80, follow these instructions:

### How to Work

1.  Read the instructions which tell you where your summary will begin and end (based on the reading passage), and exactly what you will be asked to do.
2.  Reread the part of the passage that you will have to summarize.
3.  Write a list of "main points" in note form. Do not include any unnecessary facts.

4. Connect your points to produce a *rough draft* of the summary in your own words. Refer to the passage only when you want to make sure of some point. Do not count the number of words in your summary until you have finished your rough draft.

5. In the rough draft, it is likely that you will go well over the word limit. Go over your draft carefully for possible errors, and bring the number of words down to the maximum word limit. You may write fewer than 80 words, but you should never write more.

6. Write a *final copy* of your summary, marking down the exact number of words you have used.

7. Give your summary a title.

Work through the examples given below and note how each exercise or assignment has been done.

### Example

The total number of cars in the United States now exceeds 130,000,000. Traffic goes on increasing all the time and the streets of most big cities are almost permanently blocked by a slow-moving procession of

5   vehicles. Complicated systems of one-way streets and the universal use of traffic lights have not provided a real solution to the problem. As far as the person behind the wheel is concerned, driving in crowded cities is far from being a pleasure.

10   Some time ago, a friend of mine, who works in a part of the city I do not know very well, invited me to meet with him in his office. It took me over an hour to get there and I drove around and around looking for a parking place. Finally, I found a spot on a back street.

15   Since I was already late for the appointment, I parked my car quickly and hurried off on foot. Making my way rapidly along the street, I could not help reflecting that, nowadays, it is much easier to walk than to drive.

At noon, just as I was leaving my friend's office, it

20   suddenly struck me that I had no idea where I had parked my car. I could hardly go up to a policeman and tell him that I had lost a small green car some-

where! I would simply have to look for it myself. Walking down street after street, I examined each car
25 closely and after a quarter of an hour or so was relieved to see a small green car just behind an old truck. But how disappointed I was to discover that although the car was exactly like my own, it belonged to someone else! Feeling quite tired now, I gave up
30 the search for the time being and went off to have lunch. Some time later, I left the restaurant and walked idly down the street. Turning a corner, I nearly jumped for joy: my car was right in front of me—and there was no mistaking it this time. I could not help
35 smiling as I walked over to it. Attached to the windshield wiper was a ticket which informed me that the car had been visited by a policeman in my absence. To add to all of my troubles, I was now going to have to pay a parking fine!

## 1. Comprehension

In your own words, give short answers to these questions. Give one complete sentence for each answer.

    (a) Why are the streets of most big cities almost permanently blocked?

    (b) What did the writer do after he arrived close to his friend's office?

    (c) Why was the writer in a hurry when he parked his car?

## 2. Vocabulary

Give another word or phrase to replace the following words and phrases as they are used in the passage: exceeds (2); increasing (2); permanently (4); universal (6); pleasure (9); a spot (14); reflecting (17).

## 3. Summary

In not more than 80 words, describe the writer's experiences after he left his friend's office. Use your own words. Do not include anything that is not in the last paragraph of the reading (Lines 19 to 39).

## 4. Essay

Write a composition in about 250 words on *one* of the following:

    (a)   Imagine that the writer's search had proven to be even more difficult. Write an account of the writer's search for his car.

    (b)   Pretend that you were driving the car and could not find anywhere to park. Describe what you did.

## Possible answers

## 1. Comprehension

    (a)   The streets of most big cities are almost permanently blocked because the number of cars is growing all the time.

    (b)   After he arrived close to his friend's office, the writer tried to find a place to park his car.

    (c)   The writer was in a hurry when he parked his car because he was already late for his appointment.

## 2. Vocabulary

exceeds: is more than
increasing: growing more and more
permanently: continuously
universal: general
pleasure: joy
a spot: a parking place
reflecting: thinking

## 3. Summary

## Main Points

1. Could not remember.
2. Walked down street after street.

3. Examined each car.
4. Saw small green one.
5. Same—but someone else's.
6. Gave up search.
7. Went for lunch.
8. Left restaurant.
9. Walked down street.
10. Turned down street.
11. Saw ticket—windshield—police.

**Rough Draft**

Because the writer could not remember where he had left his car, he walked down street after street looking carefully at all the parked cars. Finally, he saw a small green one which was just the same as his, but which belonged to someone else. Then he gave up the search and went to a restaurant for lunch. He left the restaurant some time later and walked down the street. When he turned the corner, he suddenly found his car. As he got closer, he noticed that there was a ticket on the windshield.

(95 Words)

**Final Copy**

*Car Problems*

Unable to remember where he had parked, the writer went down street after street looking carefully at each car. Finally, he saw a small green one which looked like his own but which belonged to someone else. Then he gave up the search and went to lunch. On leaving the restaurant some time later, he walked down the street and suddenly found his car just around the corner. As he got closer, he noticed a ticket on the windshield.

(79 Words)

## 71

It was the morning of a new day on the Moon. The Sun was low in the sky, about twenty degrees above the horizon. Astronauts Alan B. Shepard, Jr. and Edgar D. Mitchell were climbing a steep slope.
5 Their maps indicated that they were approaching their destination, the rim of Cone Crater, where they expected to find some unusual rocks that might be scientific treasures. Walking on the Moon is easy because men and their backpacks weigh only one-
10 sixth as much as they do on Earth. But uphill movement in a bulky spacesuit limits mobility and can be exhausting.

"You know we haven't reached the rim yet," said Apollo 14 Commander Shepard. "I'm not sure that
15 was Flank Crater we were in a minute ago either," replied Astronaut Mitchell. "Wait a minute. The rim's right here. That's Flank Crater over there, and that's the east shoulder running down from Cone Crater. We're going to hit it on the south side."
20 The rhythmic sounds of the astronauts' breathing were picked up by the built-in microphones of their helmets and could be heard a quarter of a million miles away at Mission Control in Houston, Texas. Also hearing them were millions of radio listeners and
25 television viewers on every continent. When Shepard and Mitchell reached the top of the ridge, their disappointment was communicated to Mission

Control and their radio and television audience. The
first hint of disillusionment came from Mitchell. "Oh
30 boy . . .!" he said as he got his first look above the
ridge. "We got fooled on that one." Shepard
explained what had happened. "We were looking at
Flank Crater. The top of it wasn't the rim of Cone
Crater. You can sure be deceived by slopes here. The
35 Sun angle is very deceiving." By the best estimates
the astronauts could make, Cone Crater was still a
thirty-minute walk away. "I don't think we'll have time
to go up there," said Shepard. More than two hours
had elapsed since the men had opened the hatch on
40 their landing vehicle Antares for that second Moon
walk. According to the lunar travel schedule, the time
had come to think about turning around and heading
back.

### 1. Comprehension

Using your own words, give short answers to these
questions. Use one complete sentence for each
answer.
    (a)  How did the astronauts know they were near-
ing their destination?
    (b)  Where did the astronauts expect to find un-
usual rocks?
    (c)  Why is walking on the Moon easy?

### 2. Vocabulary

Give another word or phrase to replace the following words as they are used in the passage: climbing
(4); approaching (5); rim (6); exhausting (12); reached
(13); sure (14); hit it (19).

### 3. Summary

In not more than 80 words, describe what happened
when astronauts Shepard and Mitchell thought they
had reached the rim of Cone Crater. Use your own
words as much as possible. Do not include anything
that is not in the last paragraph of the reading (Lines
20-43).

## 4. Essay

Write a composition in about 250 words on *one* of the following:

(a) Imagine that the astronauts found the rim of Cone Crater. Describe what happened when they found some unusual rocks (and describe the rocks).

(b) Write an imaginary account of two astronauts who are lost (on the Moon) and are trying to find their way back to their landing vehicle. (Pretend you are one of the astronauts and use first-person forms.)

**72**

Animals are seldom officially employed, so it was strange to learn that a cat was formally appointed as a staff member in a government department of a tiny foreign country. The cat, called Peta, is classed as an
5 industrial civil servant and earns a salary of 780 Boltons (about $32.20) per year. She got the job because the cat employed before her had died and because she has a fine reputation. As a member of the Department of Agriculture said, "Though still young,
10 she has already caught several mice on the farm where she was born."

Peta was flown to the capital city of the country, traveling as excess baggage. When she arrived at the State Department, she received very special treat-
15 ment. Even a movie star might have envied her. A government official took time off to welcome her and the number of reporters and photographers permitted at the official reception was limited so as not to frighten her.

20 Sitting on a large executive desk, Peta looked over her shoulders at photographers. She was not in the least disturbed by flashbulbs and the questions asked by reporters. Quite at ease, she looked up at them with her big yellow eyes as if to ask what all the excite-
25 ment was about. Just then, a reporter took a toy gray

mouse from his pocket, wound it up and placed it on the desk. The mouse began to run in circles, until Peta gave it a sharp blow with her paw and sent it flying off the desk. Everybody expected her to run after it, but
30 she remained quite still. It was clear that she could not be deceived by a mechanical mouse. Suddenly she jumped off the desk and walked around the room. Reporters felt sure she must be looking for a mouse hole. Instead, however, she began to yawn and stretch
35 in a ray of sunlight coming in through the window. Everyone decided that she must be tired after her long journey, and she was taken downstairs to her special basket. But Peta soon discovered that she had a great deal of work to do, for with no cat around for several
40 weeks, the mice had been playing happily in all the government offices.

## 1. Comprehension

Using your own words, give short answers to these questions. Use one complete sentence for each answer.

(a) Why was it strange to learn that a cat was formally appointed as a staff member in a government department?

(b) What qualifications did Peta have for the job?

(c) Why might a movie star have envied Peta when she arrived in the capital city of the country?

## 2. Vocabulary

Give another word or phrase to replace the following words as they are used in the passage: seldom (1); learn (2); formally (2); salary (5); excess (13); envied (15); frighten (19).

## 3. Summary

In not more than 80 words, describe what Peta did during her meeting with reporters and photographers. Use your own words as much as possible. Do not include anything that is not in the last paragraph of the reading (Lines 20-41).

## 4. Essay

Write a composition in about 250 words on *one* of the following:

(a) Describe a day in Peta's life at the State Department.

(b) Imagine that Peta could tell her own story. How would she describe her first day in the capital city of this tiny foreign country?

George Dexter stood motionless for several minutes at the front door, his hand grasping the doorknob. "This was just too much!" he thought to himself. That other time was bad enough when he had
5 to keep it a secret from his wife right up until the night before the launch. But to ask him to take on this one without telling his wife at all was not fair to Susie. Susie had a right . . .

Just then the door suddenly opened and there was
10 Susan. "George!" she exclaimed. "It's you! You scared me to death! I heard noises out here and I . . ." "I'm sorry," George said. He stepped in and pushed the door closed behind him. "Did you miss me today?" he asked as he embraced his wife. "Well, of
15 course," Susan said. Then pushing him away gently, she studied his face carefully and asked, "What's the matter, George? Is something wrong?" "Everything's fine," he said quickly. "Everything's just great!" George took off his cap and dropped it on the hall
20 table, then he walked over to the closet to hang up his jacket. "You're worried about something," Susan said. "I can always tell." Then dismissing it she turned and started toward the kitchen. "Dinner's about ready. You hungry . . .?" George hesitated a moment.
25 "To tell you the truth, I'm not," he said, thinking to himself, "Be careful or you'll give it away. If she suspects you've already eaten over at the base, she'll know something's up." Each time a new mission is scheduled, the crew always gets a special diet the last

30 twenty-four hours. "You're not hungry?" She glanced at him for an instant in disbelief, then disappeared into the kitchen.

Susan was too preoccupied with her own thoughts to wonder why George was not starved as usual at
35 dinnertime. "How am I ever going to break it to him?" she thought. She hated the idea of being away from George for three full weeks. Her mother was not well, so of course she needed her, but why did she promise her mother she would fly to Iowa in the morning? Why
40 not Saturday morning, or even Monday? It was not fair to George. He needed her too. "You all right . . .?" George asked. Susan looked startled. She had been staring vacantly at the oven door and did not realize that he had followed her into the kitchen.
45 "Of course!" she said. "I'm fine. Everything's just fine!"

## 1. Comprehension

Using your own words, give short answers to these questions. Use one complete sentence for each answer.
- (a) What is George Dexter's profession and what was it he was not supposed to tell his wife?
- (b) Why was Susan frightened when George came home?
- (c) Why did George eat dinner at the base instead of waiting until he got home?

## 2. Vocabulary

Give another word or phrase to replace the following words and phrases as they are used in the reading passage: motionless (1); to take on this one (6); studied his face (16); dropped it (19); scheduled (29); glanced (30); disappeared into the kitchen (31).

## 3. Summary

In not more than 80 words, describe what George was thinking about (to himself) when he came home and, also, what Susan was thinking about that she hesitated telling George. Use your own words as much as possible. Do not include anything that is not in the reading passage.

### 4. Essay

Write a composition in about 250 words on *one* of the following:

   (a)  Write an imaginary account of the briefing session George Dexter had with his Flight Director when George was told about his new space flight mission.

   (b)  Imagine that Susan guessed that George was going on a secret space flight the next day and that she asked him to tell her all the details. Continue the story given in the reading passage.

According to the newspaper advertisement, the house was a two-minute walk from the bus stop, in excellent condition, and built high up on a hill, with a glorious view of the ocean. A real estate agent had
5  recommended the rooming house to me, telling me that the room rent was reasonable and that the landlady was a very pleasant person.

I calculated I had been walking for roughly fifteen minutes before I finally reached the house. It was at

10 the very edge of a barren cliff, with a sheer drop to jagged rocks below. The view of the ocean was undeniably beautiful, but I was surprised to find that the fence around the property was old and broken down, and even more surprised to discover that the yard was
15 neglected and full of weeds. When I rang the bell, a woman appeared at a window and rudely asked me what I wanted. Her sour expression turned into a smile of welcome the moment I explained that I was interested in renting a room.
20 Inside, the house had a musty smell and I immediately felt that my trip had been a waste of time. However, I followed the woman into a room at the back of the house. As soon as she opened the door, we were greeted by a cold wind that was blowing in fiercely
25 through a broken window. The plaster on the walls was cracked and the ceiling was badly spotted and stained. All of a sudden I noticed a door in one corner of the room and asked where it led to. As I got nearer to it, I was astonished to find that someone had
30 scratched a name in big letters on the door frame. The woman did not seem eager to open the door, but I insisted so much that finally she unlocked it. What I saw was the final blow! I was sure I didn't want to rent a room there. The door led to a small enclosed yard in
35 which there was the biggest collection of garbage I have ever seen: old tires, newspapers, bottles, cans, decaying shoes and clothes, and an old water pump that was completely rusted. I hurriedly thanked the woman for the trouble she had taken and left the
40 "delightful oceanfront rooming house" as quickly as I could.

## 1. Comprehension

Using your own words, give short answers to these questions. Use one complete sentence for each answer.

(a) Why did the real estate agent recommend this house to the writer?

(b) Why was the writer surprised when he got near the house?

(c) What happened when the writer rang the bell?

## 2. Vocabulary

Give another word or phrase to replace the following words and phrases as they are used in the reading passage: in excellent condition (2-3); glorious (4); reasonable (6); calculated (8); edge (10); undeniably (11-12); neglected (15).

## 3. Summary

In not more than 80 words, describe what the writer saw and did after he entered the house. Use your own words as much as possible. Do not include anything that is not in the last paragraph of the reading (Lines 20-41).

## 4. Essay

Write a composition in about 250 words on *one* of the following:
(a) Pretend that the writer rented the room he saw. Describe his life in the rooming house.
(b) Imagine that the landlady decided to write a letter to her sister describing the writer's visit. Write the letter for her (use first-person forms).

Many tourists have dreamed of owning a small house in a foreign country—perhaps on a stretch of lonely coast—to which they could return year after year to enjoy the sun and the ocean. Some visitors to
5 overseas areas, with even bigger ideas and a lot more money to spend, think of buying hotels. In buying real estate, however, it is absolutely essential to know a great deal about the value of a particular piece of property—otherwise, the buyer may be at the mercy of
10 dishonest salespeople.

Some tourists are so foolish that they almost deserve the swindles they get trapped in. We would consider a person a bit naive if he or she walked into a museum and asked to buy a great work of art.
15 Although no one has told us, we all know that certain things can never be bought, no matter how much money is offered. Yet nearly every year since 1944, a buyer has been found for the Colosseum in Rome. The first one was a soldier who parted with his money
20 for what was described as "a rather broken down and heavily damaged building . . . in a good location."

The people of Rome eagerly look forward to each year's "sale." They were amused to learn that, as usual, a tourist recently expressed the desire to buy
25 the historic building. Two real estate agents told him that the building was in need of repair, but that the buyer could expect a high return on his investment. They took him to the Colosseum itself and pointed out that the top floor would make a wonderful
30 international restaurant. It was in an ideal location and offered a fine view of the city of Rome. Besides, for some strange reason, so many people wished to visit the building that the buyer could make a handsome profit by just charging admission to
35 visitors. In the agents' opinion, it was well worth spending money on a building like this. They asked the buyer for a mere 500,000 lire as a deposit and told him they would complete arrangements that evening at a certain hotel. The tourist was sure that he had
40 bought a valuable piece of property at a bargain price and later went to the hotel to meet the real estate brokers. But, of course, the two men were not really brokers and they never showed up.

## 1. Comprehension

Using your own words, give short answers to these questions. Use one complete sentence for each answer.

    (a)   Why should tourists who want to buy a house somewhere overseas know a great deal about the value of property?

    (b)   Why would we consider a person naive if he or she walked into a museum and asked to buy a great work of art?

    (c)   Who was the first person to "buy" the Colosseum?

## 2. Vocabulary

Give another word or phrase to replace the following words as they are used in the reading passage: owning (1); foreign (2); essential (7); property (9); trapped (12); location (21).

## 3. Summary

In not more than 80 words, describe what happened when a tourist expressed the wish to "buy" the Colosseum. Use your own words as much as possible. Do not include anything that is not in the last paragraph of the reading (Lines 22 to 43).

## 4. Essay

Write a composition in about 250 words on *one* of the following:

    (a)   Imagine that the tourist had really bought the Colosseum and was free to do with it as he pleased. Describe what happened.

    (b)   Imagine that the agents went to the hotel that evening to meet the tourist again as arranged. Continue the story given in the reading.

The writers of murder mysteries go to a great deal of trouble to keep us guessing right up to the end. In actual fact, people often behave more strangely in real life than they do in stories.

5    The following personal notice once appeared in the classified ads of a local newspaper: "An opportunity to earn $750. A man . . . willing to take chances wanted for an out-of-the-ordinary job which needs to be performed only once and which will take just a few

10  minutes." A reader found this generous offer irresist-
ible and replied to the post office box number given in
the ad—but being a bit suspicious, he gave a false
name. Soon afterwards, he received a reply. Enclosed
in the envelope was a typed note instructing him to
15  call a certain number if he was still interested. He
called the number and found out that the man in the
ad wanted him to "get rid of somebody" and would
discuss it more fully with him the next day. But the
man who had replied to the ad got in touch with the
20  police and from then on acted under their instructions.

The police saw the two men meet and watched
them as they drove away together. In the car the man
who had placed the ad came to the point at once: he
25  told the man he wanted him to shoot his wife. The
reason he gave was that he was suffering from an
incurable disease and wanted to move to a warmer
climate, but his wife objected to this. Giving the man
some money, he instructed him to buy a gun and
30  warned him to be careful of the dog which, though it
would not bite, might bark a lot and attract the
attention of neighbors. He also gave him a
photograph of his wife so that he would be able to
recognize her. After that, he suggested that the man
35  "do the job" the next morning. Meanwhile, he would
prepare his wife by telling her that a young man was
going to stop by the house. After the murder, they
would meet again outside a bus station and the
money would be paid as arranged. The second
40  meeting never took place because shortly after this
first meeting, the man who had been planning to have
his wife murdered was arrested.

### 1. Comprehension

Using your own words, give short answers to these
questions. Use one complete sentence for each
answer.

   (a)  What do the writers of murder stories try to do?
   (b)  What sort of person did the advertisement in
        the newspaper ask for?

(c) Why did the reader give a false name when he answered the ad?

## 2. Vocabulary

Give another word or phrase to replace the following words as they are used in the reading passage: behave (3); opportunity (6); being (12); a bit (12); false (12); reply (13); discuss (18).

## 3. Summary

In not more than 80 words, write an account of what the man who had placed the ad told the other man after they drove away together. Use your own words as much as possible. Do not include anything that is not in the last paragraph of the reading passage (Lines 22 to 42).

## 4. Essay

Write a composition in about 250 words on *one* of the following:

(a) Imagine that the man referred to in the passage had not gone to the police and that he had agreed to do what the man in the ad wanted. Describe what happened.

(b) Describe how the man who placed the ad was arrested by the police. Write an imaginary account of what he told them.

**77**

I lose so many things that I could swear they just get up and walk away by themselves. Perhaps I have never admitted it—even to myself—but I am extremely jealous of people who are so organized and careful
5 that they never lose anything. Most of my friends seem to have a place for everything, and things are always where they should be. I hate comparing myself with them. They have special cabinets for tools, hooks to hang things on and drawers to put things in. It is

10 quite impossible for me to compete with people like this.

Some things have a terrible habit of making themselves scarce the moment I need them. Pencils and ballpoint pens are never anywhere near the telephone
15 when it rings, no matter how much care I seem to take. Screwdrivers and can openers always manage to wander out into the yard someplace and as a result, loose screws in things do not get tightened and opening cans is always a big problem. Needles
20 disappear every time I want to sew a button on a shirt, and of course spools of thread always get lost somewhere.

The situation was getting so out of control that I decided I'd better get organized. I had a large cabinet
25 built in the kitchen. On the shelves I neatly arranged a number of boxes and tin cans, the contents of which I clearly marked on the outside. I had a box for pins, another for nails, and a special place for screwdrivers, hammers and wrenches. There was a new address
30 book in one corner of the cabinet so that I could conveniently jot down telephone numbers and addresses. Before this I had always written addresses on bits of paper—which promptly got lost. Soon everything was neatly arranged in its place, from
35 scissors to cakes of soap and spare light bulbs. Having made such a sincere attempt to prevent things from running away, I felt very proud of myself. But it was not long before the matches disappeared and the hammer decided to hide itself in the wastepaper
40 basket. I soon got my revenge, however; I had a lock installed on the cabinet doors and thus made sure that nothing could escape. This was a perfect solution —until I lost the key to the lock!

### 1. Comprehension

Using your own words, give short answers to these questions. Use one complete sentence for each answer.

(a) Why does the writer hate comparing himself with others?

    (b)   When does the writer need pencils and ball-point pens?

    (c)   Why do loose screws stay that way and why does the writer have a problem opening cans?

## 2. Vocabulary

Give another word or phrase to replace the following words and phrases as they are used in the reading passage: jealous (4); organized (4); hate (7); compete (10); making themselves scarce (12); the moment (13); wander (17); disappear (20).

## 3. Summary

In not more than 80 words, describe what steps the writer took to prevent things from disappearing. Use your own words as much as possible. Do not include anything that is not in the last paragraph of the reading (Lines 23-43).

## 4. Essay

Write a composition in about 250 words on *one* of the following:

    (a)   Describe how the writer found the key to the cabinet and how, in a short time, he managed to lose everything in it. (Use first-person forms in your composition.)

    (b)   Describe your own experiences in not being able to find things you need.

These days we are so accustomed to telegrams that it is hard for us to imagine the excitement that must have been felt when the first telegraph cables were laid in the nineteenth century.

5    Cable laying proved to be immensely difficult. The cable which in the fall of 1850 carried the first telegraph messages between England and France had a very short life. The day after its inauguration, a fisherman "caught" the cable by mistake. Thinking that the
10  copper wire at the center of the thick cable was gold, he cut a piece off to show to his friends. However, a

new cable was put down, and soon news could travel quickly across Europe. But there was still no way of sending messages between Europe and America.

15   When the Atlantic Telegraph Company was formed in 1856, a serious attempt was made to "join" Europe to America with no less than 2,300 miles of cable. Since no one ship could carry that much weight, the job was shared by two sailing vessels, the
20 *Agamemnon* and the *Niagara*. After setting out from opposite directions, the intention was that they should meet in the middle of the Atlantic Ocean where the two cables would be connected together. But the ships had hardly covered 300 miles when the cable
25 broke. In 1858, a second attempt was made. This time the ships were hindered by storms and were again unsuccessful. A few months later, there was great rejoicing when—after the combined efforts of both ships—England and the United States were at last
30 connected by cable and the Queen of England was able to speak to the President of the United States. This cable, however, only lasted eleven weeks. Further attempts were postponed until 1864 when Brunel's steamship, the *Great Eastern,* set forth. This
35 powerful ship did the whole job by itself, but again messages could not travel freely because the cable developed a fault. While it was being repaired, it broke and 1,300 miles of it lay on the ocean floor. Finally, however, two years later, the *Great Eastern* completed
40 a highly successful journey, and since then, it has been possible to send messages to all parts of the world.

### 1.  Comprehension

Using your own words, give short answers to these questions. Use one complete sentence for each answer.

(a)   When was the first telegraph cable laid?

(b)   Why did the fisherman think that the cable he had "caught" was valuable?

(c)   How many miles of cable were needed to join Europe to America?

## 2. Vocabulary

Give another word or phrase to replace the following words and phrases as they are used in the reading passage: accustomed to (1); hard (2); laid (4); immensely (5); by mistake (9); at the center (10); way (13).

## 3. Summary

In not more than 80 words, describe how a cable was laid between England and the United States, from line 23 (But the ships . . .) to the end. Use your own words as much as possible. Do not include anything that is not in the last paragraph of the reading (Lines 15 to 42).

## 4. Essay

Write a composition in about 250 words on *one* of the following:
- (a) Write an imaginary account of the third successful journey of the sailing vessels *Agamemnon* and *Niagara*.
- (b) Imagine the fisherman "catching" the cable. Write a first-person account of what happened.

In the twentieth century, numerous new nations have been formed. Though their people enjoy full political liberty, in a few of these countries there exists at the same time a number of unusual
5 practices. People may be free to vote and to elect whoever they please to govern them, but certain popular prejudices and old customs take a long time to die out. However, now that people have new opportunities, they need not suffer in silence because
10 they can now express their views openly. With rapid economic development, improved living conditions, and the widespread availability of radios, books and newspapers, most people are fairly well informed. In

this way, certain traditional practices have begun to
15 disappear rapidly.

There was a good example of this not too long ago in a newly formed republic when a girl of fourteen refused to marry a sixty-year-old man who had "bought" her for the equivalent of $100. Her father
20 had agreed to the marriage when the girl was only four years old and had "sold" her to a man who already had at least six wives. Just before the marriage ceremony, the girl ran away and wrote to the president of the republic. In her letter she pointed out
25 that although her country was independent, its people were still not truly free. Some human beings were like slaves, she said, and women could be bought and sold like cattle. She asked the president if he felt that this was right. This letter caused the president a great
30 deal of concern and he immediately took steps to change the traditional law which permitted women to be bought and sold.

The girl had won a considerable victory but she still had a big problem. She had to find $100 to repay the
35 man who might have become her husband. There seemed to be no way of raising so much money. Fortunately, however, the girl's story was broadcast in a radio program in several countries and nearly $5,000 poured in from listeners. The buyer got his money
40 back and the girl was free to marry anyone she chose. She had won true freedom for herself and for others like her.

## 1. Comprehension

Using your own words, give short answers to these questions. Use one complete sentence for each answer.

(a) What sometimes prevents people from enjoying true freedom?

(b) What has been the effect of the spread of education and the improvement of living conditions?

(c) Who was the girl "sold" to?

## 2. Vocabulary

Give another word or phrase to replace the following words and phrases as they are used in the passage: nations (1); liberty (3); elect (5); please (6); to die out (8); views (10); improved (11).

## 3. Summary

In not more than 80 words, describe what the girl did to win her freedom and explain how money was collected to pay back the man who had "bought" her. Use your own words as much as possible. Do not include anything that is not in the last two paragraphs of the reading passage (Lines 16 to 42).

## 4. Essay

Write a composition in about 250 words on *one* of the following:
- (a) Write an account of the broadcast which brought in money to help the girl.
- (b) Imagine yourself in the girl's position. Write a letter to the president of the republic.

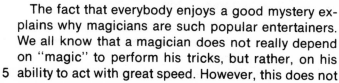

The fact that everybody enjoys a good mystery explains why magicians are such popular entertainers. We all know that a magician does not really depend on "magic" to perform his tricks, but rather, on his
5 ability to act with great speed. However, this does not

prevent us from enjoying a magician who can produce rabbits from a hat, swallow countless eggs or saw his wife in two.

Probably the greatest magician of all time was Harry
10 Houdini. He died in 1926. His real name was Ehrich Weiss, but he adopted the name "Houdini" after reading a book which influenced him greatly. The book was written by a famous magician called Robert-Houdin. Houdini mastered the art of escaping. He
15 could free himself from the tightest knots or the most complicated locks in just seconds. Although no one really knows how he did these things, there is no doubt that he had made a close study of every type of lock ever invented. Strapped to his leg, he carried a
20 small needlelike tool made of steel, and it is believed that he used this tool in place of a key.

Houdini once asked the Chicago police to lock him up in prison. They bound him in chains and locked him up, but he freed himself in an instant. The police
25 accused him of having used some kind of tool, and they locked him up again. This time he wore no clothes and there were chains around his neck, waist, wrists and legs; but he again escaped in a few minutes. The usual explanation is that Houdini had
30 probably hidden his "needle" in a waxlike substance and dropped it on the floor somewhere in a passageway. As he went past, then, he could have stepped on it so that it would stick to the bottom of his foot. Houdini's most famous escape, however, was
35 altogether astonishing. He was heavily chained and enclosed in an empty wooden chest—the lid of which was nailed. The chest was then dropped into the water in New York Harbor. One minute later, Houdini returned to the surface. When the chest was brought
40 up, it was opened and the chains were found inside.

## 1. Comprehension

Using your own words, give short answers to these questions. Use one complete sentence for each answer.

(a) Why are magicians such popular entertainers?

(b) Why did Weiss adopt the name of "Houdini"?

(c) What did Houdini use to open locks?

## 2. Vocabulary

Give another word or phrase to replace the following words and phrases as they are used in the passage: popular (2); prevent (6); produce (7); saw (8); influenced (12); escaping (14); in place of (21).

## 3. Summary

In not more than 80 words, give an account of Houdini's experiences as described in the last paragraph of the reading.

Use your own words as much as possible.

## 4. Essay

Write a composition in about 250 words on *one* of the following:

(a) Describe what Houdini did inside the chest after it was dropped into the water in New York Harbor. (Use your imagination.)

(b) Describe a performance that you once saw given by a magician.